GILDED AGE

REVEALED

Untold Stories of Opulent Mansions,
Scandalous Power Plays, and Groundbreaking
Inventions Unveiled in a Matter of Days

Lennon
Publishing

Second Edition, 2025

Contents

Note To The Reader

T hank you for picking up the Expanded Edition of *Gilded Age Revealed: Untold Stories of Opulent Mansions, Scandalous Power Plays, and Groundbreaking Inventions Unveiled in a Matter of Days*

Your enthusiasm for the original release inspired us to create something extra for this edition, a nod to the vibrancy and spirit of the era. Alongside the full original content, you'll find a special bonus feature celebrating the sights, sounds, and tastes of the Gilded Age.

Whether you're returning for another glimpse into high society or stepping into this dazzling world for the first time, we invite you to settle in, linger over the stories, and let your imagination roam through the opulence, intrigue, and invention that defined a generation.

Expanded Edition, 2025

Introduction

The year is 1883, and the streets of New York City are alive with energy. Horse-drawn carriages clatter over cobblestone roads, while street vendors shout their wares. The air is thick with the mingling scents of fresh bread, coal smoke, and the salty breeze from the harbor. On one side of the street, towering mansions flaunt their grandeur, their opulent facades a testament to the vast wealth of their owners. On the other side, tenement buildings stand in stark contrast, crowded with families struggling to make ends meet. This is the Gilded Age, a time of stark contrasts and breathtaking change.

Why should we care about the Gilded Age today? This period, spanning from the 1870s to about 1900, is crucial for understanding modern America. The Gilded Age gave birth to many of the economic disparities, political systems, and cultural norms we see today. Think of the construction of the Brooklyn Bridge, a marvel of engineering that connected communities and symbolized the era's ambition. Or consider the invention of the electric light bulb by Thomas Edison, which transformed night into day and revolutionized the way people lived and worked.

In this book, we will explore the many facets of the Gilded Age. We will delve into the technological advancements that defined the era, from the railroads that crisscrossed the nation to the skyscrapers that began to touch the sky. We will also examine the social changes, including the rise of labor unions and the fight for women's rights. Key figures like Andrew Carnegie, John D. Rockefeller, and J.P. Morgan will come to life, their ambitions and actions illuminating the era. While we will marvel at the opulence and innovation, we won't shy away from the controversies and challenges that marked the time—economic inequality, political corruption, and social unrest.

The central argument of this book is that while the Gilded Age was an era of great progress and prosperity, it also sowed the seeds of many modern challenges. Economic inequality and corporate dominance, issues we grapple with today, have their roots in this period. By understanding the Gilded Age, we can gain insights into our current struggles and perhaps find clues for addressing them.

My fascination with the Gilded Age began years ago, driven by a desire not just to recount historical facts but to make the era come alive for you. I want to transport you back in time with a narrative that is both engaging and informative. As you read, you'll find yourself walking the bustling streets of New York City, dining in opulent ballrooms, and witnessing the groundbreaking innovations that changed the world.

This book draws from various disciplines, including economics, sociology, and art history, to provide a well-rounded view of the Gilded Age. This multidisciplinary approach will help you understand the complex nature of the period. You'll see how economic theories, social movements, and artistic expressions all intertwined to shape an era of contrasts and transformations.

The Gilded Age is not just a chapter in a history book; it's a mirror reflecting many of the issues we face today. Economic disparities, political corruption, and social reforms were as relevant then as they are now. By drawing parallels between the past and the present, this book aims to show how the lessons of the Gilded Age can help us navigate our current challenges.

The book is structured to take you on a journey from the innovations and opulence of the era to the societal shifts and pivotal roles of key figures. We'll start with the technological marvels and industrial giants, move through the social changes and reform movements, and finally explore the lasting legacy of the Gilded Age. This structure will help you understand how the different elements of the era fit together and influenced each other.

As you turn the pages, I invite you to consider this: What lessons does the Gilded Age hold for us today? How can understanding this period help us address the economic and social issues we face? The answers may surprise you, and they may offer valuable insights for our time.

So, let's step into the past together. The adventure awaits.

One: The Dawn of Industrial Majesty

In the late 1800s, America was a land of booming industry and relentless progress. Imagine standing on a bustling factory floor, the air filled with the clang of machinery and the shouts of foremen. Workers, their faces smeared with grime, move with precision and haste, each contributing to a machine that seems almost alive with energy. This was the heartbeat of the Gilded Age—a period of rapid industrialization that transformed the American landscape and economy. It was a time when titans of industry like Andrew Carnegie and John D. Rockefeller built empires that would leave lasting legacies, not just in brick and steel, but in the very fabric of American society.

The Gilded Age was a period of incredible innovation and expansion. It saw the rise of skyscrapers, the spread of railroads, and the advent of electric lighting—each of these advancements reshaping the way people lived and worked. But it was also an era of stark contrasts: immense wealth sat alongside deep poverty, and groundbreaking progress was accompanied by significant social strife. This chapter will take you through the monumental changes that defined this era, beginning with one of its most influential figures: Andrew Carnegie.

The Steel Spine of America: How Andrew Carnegie's Innovations Shaped the Nation

Andrew Carnegie's story is one of ambition, innovation, and a relentless drive for success. Born in Scotland in 1835, Carnegie immigrated to the United States with his family, settling in Pittsburgh. He began working at a young age, starting as a bobbin boy in a cotton factory and later becoming a telegraph operator. His keen intellect and tireless work ethic caught the attention of Thomas Scott of the Pennsylvania Railroad, who became a mentor to Carnegie. Through Scott, Carnegie learned the intricacies of the railroad business and began investing in iron and steel, laying the groundwork for what would become a colossal empire.

One of Carnegie's most significant contributions to the industrial age was his adoption of the Bessemer process. Developed by Henry Bessemer in England, this method allowed for the mass production of steel by blowing air through molten iron to remove impurities. The result was a stronger and more durable metal that could be produced at a fraction of the cost. Carnegie recognized the potential of this process and invested heavily in it, transforming his steel mills into some of the most efficient and productive in the world. This innovation drastically reduced the cost of steel production, making it possible to construct the towering skyscrapers and expansive railroads that came to define American cities.

Carnegie's business strategies were as innovative as his approach to steelmaking. He was a pioneer of vertical integration, a practice that involved controlling every aspect of the production process—from raw materials to distribution. This strategy allowed Carnegie to reduce costs and increase efficiency, as he no longer had to rely on external suppliers. He acquired iron ore mines, coal fields, and even railroads, ensuring that every step of the production process was under his control. This boosted his profits and set a new standard for business practices in America, influencing industries far beyond steel.

Carnegie's legacy, however, extends beyond his industrial achievements. As his wealth grew, so did his commitment to philanthropy. He believed in the "Gospel of Wealth," the idea that the rich had a moral obligation to use their wealth for the greater good. True to his word, Carnegie donated millions of dollars to build public libraries, universities, and cultural institutions. By the time of his death, he had given away more than $350 million, a staggering sum at the time. His contributions helped to democratize access to knowledge and education, leaving a lasting impact on American society.

Yet, Carnegie's industrial practices were not without controversy, particularly when it came to labor. The conditions in his steel mills were harsh, with long hours, low wages, and dangerous working environments. Tensions between labor and management came to a head during the Homestead Strike of 1892, one of the most significant labor conflicts of the era. Workers at the Homestead Steel Works, frustrated by wage cuts and poor working conditions, went on strike. The conflict escalated into a violent confrontation between strikers and private security forces, resulting in deaths on both sides. The strike was eventually broken, but it left a lasting stain on Carnegie's reputation and highlighted the deep divisions between capital and labor in the Gilded Age.

Carnegie's story is a complex one, marked by incredible achievements and significant controversies. His innovations in steelmaking and business practices transformed industries and laid the groundwork for modern corporate America. His philanthropic efforts helped to shape the cultural and educational landscape of the nation. Yet, the harsh realities faced by his workers and the conflicts that arose from his industrial practices remind us that progress often comes at a cost. As we continue to explore the Gilded Age, Carnegie's legacy serves as a lens through which we can understand the broader themes of innovation, wealth, and social change that defined this transformative period in American history.

The Railroad Tycoons: Building the Tracks that Connected a Continent

Railroads were the veins through which the lifeblood of the American economy flowed during the Gilded Age. Imagine standing at a bustling train station, the air thick with the scent of coal and steam, as trains thunder in and out, carrying passengers and freight across the country. The transformation of the American landscape by the expansion of the railroad network is one of the era's most remarkable stories. Figures like Cornelius Vanderbilt, known as the "Commodore," spearheaded this explosive growth. Vanderbilt, who initially made his fortune in shipping, turned his attention to railroads in the 1860s. By acquiring and consolidating rail lines, such as the New York Central and the Hudson River Railroad, he created an interconnected system that stretched from New York City to Chicago, fundamentally altering the nation's commerce and daily life.

One of the most significant innovations in railroad logistics during this period was the adoption of the standard gauge for tracks. Before this, different rail lines often used varying widths, or gauges, making it impossible for trains to travel seamlessly from one line to another. The standard gauge, set at 4 feet, 8.5 inches, became the norm, allowing for the efficient movement of trains across different railroad networks. This seemingly simple standardization had profound implications, facilitating the smooth transfer of goods and passengers and vastly improving the efficiency of the rail transport system. Another critical innovation was the introduction of air brakes, developed by George Westinghouse in the 1860s. Air brakes allowed trains to stop more reliably and safely, reducing the risk of accidents and enabling longer, heavier trains to operate.

The economic impact of railroads was nothing short of revolutionary. Railroads created national markets by connecting previously isolated regions, allowing goods to be transported quickly and cheaply across vast distances. This connectivity spurred the growth of other industries, particularly steel and coal, which were essential for building and fueling the railroads. The demand for steel rails and locomotives provided a significant boost to the steel industry, while coal became the primary fuel source for steam engines, driving the expansion of coal mining operations. The railroads also facilitated the movement of agricultural products from the Midwest to urban markets, transforming the American economy from one of localized production and consumption to an interconnected national system.

The social changes brought about by the railroads were equally transformative. Rail connectivity encouraged the movement of populations, with people flocking to urban centers searching for jobs and opportunities. This migration contributed to the rise of suburban living, as rail lines made it possible for people to live outside crowded city centers while still commuting to work. The railroads also transformed rural landscapes into industrial hubs. Towns that once relied solely on agriculture began to develop industries and attract businesses, leading to the growth of new communities along the rail lines.

Consider the impact on daily life: a farmer in Kansas could now sell his wheat in markets as far away as New York City, while a factory worker in Pennsylvania might receive goods from across the country. The railroads shrank the distance between places, making the vast expanse of the United States feel more connected and accessible. They also played a crucial role in the westward expansion, facilitating the movement of settlers and goods to the western territories and contributing to the growth and development of new states.

The story of the railroad tycoons and their impact on America is a testament to the transformative power of innovation and ambition. Figures like Vanderbilt not only built railroads but also laid the foundation for America's economic and social development. The legacy of the railroads is still evident today, in the interconnectedness of our markets, the structure of our cities, and the very fabric of American life.

Edison and the Age of Electricity: Illuminating the Nation's Future

Imagine a time when the streets of New York City were lit only by gas lamps and the occasional flicker of candlelight through a window. Nighttime was a shadowy affair, and productivity slowed as the sun dipped below the horizon. This all changed with Thomas Edison's invention of the electric light bulb. In 1879, Edison unveiled a practical incandescent light bulb, a breakthrough that would forever alter the fabric of daily life. The light bulb extended productive hours, transforming urban landscapes into bustling centers of activity even after dark. Factories could operate around the clock, and homes were no longer bound by the limits of daylight. The establishment of the first electric power stations, such as the Pearl Street Station in Manhattan, marked the dawn of a new era. These stations generated and distributed electricity, illuminating streets and homes, and laying the groundwork for a nation electrified.

The rapid spread of electrical infrastructure across America was nothing short of revolutionary. As power stations multiplied, so did the web of wires connecting them to homes, businesses, and factories. This electrification spurred growth in various industries. Manufacturing processes became more efficient with the introduction of electrically powered machinery. The entertainment industry also flourished, with the advent of electric theaters and later, the motion picture projector. Electric streetcars began to replace horse-drawn carriages, making urban transit faster and more reliable. The ripple effects of electrification touched every corner of society, enhancing productivity and spurring economic growth.

Edison's approach to business was as innovative as his technological creations. Understanding the importance of protecting intellectual property, he secured numerous patents for his inventions. This safeguarded his work and established a model for future inventors and entrepreneurs. In 1892, Edison's various business ventures were consolidated into the

General Electric Company (GE), a behemoth that set new standards for corporate America. GE became a leader in electrical innovation, continuously pushing the boundaries of what was possible. Edison's business model emphasized research and development, leading to an environment where innovation thrived. His strategies in patenting and corporate organization laid the groundwork for modern business practices, influencing countless industries beyond electricity.

The societal changes brought about by electricity were profound. In homes, electric lighting replaced the dim glow of oil lamps and candles, creating safer and more pleasant living environments. Kitchens and living rooms became centers of activity well into the evening, changing family dynamics and social behaviors. The ability to control light at the flick of a switch also influenced architecture, allowing for the design of buildings and homes that maximized both natural and artificial light. In workplaces, electric lighting increased productivity and improved working conditions, reducing the risk of accidents in poorly lit environments.

Electricity also transformed social behaviors and nighttime activities. The extension of the day allowed for more leisure activities in the evenings. Theaters, restaurants, and public spaces stayed open later, catering to a population that was no longer bound by the setting sun. This shift had a profound impact on urban life, making cities more vibrant and active at night. The social fabric of communities changed as people gathered in well-lit public spaces, fostering a sense of safety and community.

Edison's innovations did not just light up streets and homes—they illuminated the path to a modern, electrified world. The introduction of the electric light bulb and the spread of electricity transformed daily life, reshaped industries and set new standards for business practices. As we flip a switch to light up a room or charge our devices, we are reminded of the groundbreaking work of Edison and his contemporaries. Their contributions laid the foundation for the electrified world we live in today, a world where light is no longer a luxury but a fundamental part of our existence. The age of electricity, sparked by Edison's ingenuity, continues to illuminate our lives in ways both profound and everyday.

The Birth of Telecommunication: Alexander Graham Bell's Enduring Legacy

Imagine a world where sending a message across town required a handwritten note and a messenger. Communication was slow, cumbersome, and often unreliable. This changed dramatically with the invention of the telephone by Alexander Graham Bell, a Scottish-born inventor who immigrated to the United States. Bell, who had a keen interest in sound and speech due to his work with the deaf, was driven by the desire to transmit vocal sounds over a wire. His breakthrough came on March 10, 1876, when he famously called out to his assistant, "Mr. Watson, come here, I want to see you," through his experimental device. This moment marked the birth of a revolutionary technology that would forever alter the landscape of communication.

The telephone's technological novelty lay in its ability to convert sound into electrical signals and then back into sound. Bell's device used a diaphragm, a coil of wire, and a magnet to achieve this transformation. When a person spoke into the mouthpiece, the sound waves caused the diaphragm to vibrate. These vibrations induced a corresponding electric current in the coil, which traveled along a wire to another telephone. At the receiving end, the process was reversed, with the electrical signals causing a diaphragm to vibrate and reproduce the original sound. This ingenious mechanism allowed real-time voice communication over long distances, a feat previously unimaginable.

The early growth of the telephone network was rapid and transformative. Initially, telephones were connected directly to each other, a system known as point-to-point communication. However, as the number of users grew, this method became impractical. The solution was the creation of the central exchange, a hub where multiple lines could be connected through a switchboard operated by human operators. This innovation allowed any telephone to call any other telephone connected to the same exchange, vastly increasing the network's utility. By the end of the 19th century, long-distance connections began to emerge, linking cities and even states, further enhancing the reach and impact of the telephone.

Regulatory and patent battles were a significant aspect of the telephone's early history. Bell faced numerous challenges to his patents, with competitors seeking to capitalize on his invention. One of the most notable legal battles was with Elisha Gray, who claimed to have filed a similar patent on the same day as Bell. The ensuing court cases set important precedents for technology patents and regulatory frameworks. Bell's eventual victory secured his place in history and underscored the importance of protecting intellectual property in fostering innovation. These legal struggles highlighted the competitive nature of technological advancement and the need for clear regulatory guidelines.

The cultural impact of telecommunications was profound and far-reaching. The telephone revolutionized social interactions by shrinking the distances between people. Families could stay connected despite living miles apart, businesses could conduct transactions more efficiently, and news could spread rapidly. The telephone also played a crucial role in emergencies, enabling quick communication with authorities and medical services. This newfound ability to communicate instantly altered perceptions of distance and connectivity, making the world feel smaller and more accessible. It fostered a sense of immediacy and responsiveness that reshaped both personal and professional relationships.

Consider a bustling office in the early 20th century, where the constant ringing of telephones signals the pulse of modern business. Deals are struck, meetings are arranged, and information flows seamlessly across the wires. The telephone became an indispensable tool for industries, streamlining operations and enhancing productivity. In homes, it offered a new level of convenience and connection, allowing people to maintain relationships and manage daily affairs with unprecedented ease. The cultural shift was significant, as the telephone became a symbol of progress and modernity, reflecting the era's spirit of innovation and transformation.

The enduring legacy of Alexander Graham Bell's invention can be seen in the way we communicate today. From the early days of wired telephones to the wireless smartphones of the 21st century, the fundamental principles of Bell's invention remain at the core of our communication technologies. His work laid the foundation for a connected world, where information and voices travel at the speed of light, bridging gaps and bringing people together. The birth of telecommunication was not just a technological breakthrough; it was a cultural milestone that continues to shape our lives in ways both profoundly and every day.

The Rise of Standard Oil: John D. Rockefeller and the Oil Industry's Early Days

Picture the oil fields of Pennsylvania in the 1860s, a landscape dotted with derricks and teeming with activity. It was here that John D. Rockefeller saw an opportunity that would forever change the American economy. Born in 1839, Rockefeller was a shrewd business-man who understood that the oil industry, still in its infancy, was ripe for transformation. In 1870, he founded the Standard Oil Company with a clear vision: to dominate the oil market through efficiency, innovation, and aggressive business practices. Rockefeller's strategies would turn Standard Oil into a behemoth, controlling nearly 90% of the oil refining industry by the 1880s.

Innovative business practices and monopolistic tactics marked Rockefeller's approach to building Standard Oil. One of his most effective strategies was the use of rebates from railroads. By negotiating lower transportation costs for his company, Rockefeller could undercut his competitors on price, driving many out of business or forcing them to sell to him. This tactic reduced costs and ensured that Standard Oil could maintain a competitive edge. Additionally, Rockefeller forged strategic alliances with other oil com-panies, creating a trust that centralized control over the industry. Through acquisitions and partnerships, he systematically eliminated competition, consolidating his power and creating a near-monopoly.

The impact of Standard Oil's dominance on competitors and the broader economy was profound. Smaller oil companies struggled to survive in the face of Standard Oil's aggressive tactics. Many were bought out, while others simply couldn't compete with the lower prices and superior efficiency of Rockefeller's operations. This consolidation led to significant economies of scale, allowing Standard Oil to produce oil more cheaply and efficiently than ever before. However, it also stifled competition and innovation, as few could challenge the might of Rockefeller's empire. The broader implications for American capitalism were equally significant. Standard Oil set a blueprint for corporate monopolies, demonstrating how a combination of strategic business practices and sheer market power could create an industrial giant.

Public and governmental responses to Standard Oil's practices were mixed. On one hand, many admired Rockefeller's business acumen and the efficiency of his operations. On the other, there was growing concern about the concentration of economic power and its implications for democracy and fair competition. The 1890 Sherman Antitrust Act was a legislative response aimed at curbing monopolies and restoring competitive markets. However, it wasn't until 1906, when President Theodore Roosevelt's administration took a more aggressive stance against trusts, that Standard Oil faced serious legal challenges. The landmark 1911 Supreme Court decision ordered the breakup of Standard Oil into 34 separate companies, a move that marked a significant shift in American antitrust policy.

The breakup of Standard Oil did not diminish Rockefeller's influence or legacy. The companies that emerged from the dissolution, including ExxonMobil, Chevron, and Amoco, continued to be major players in the oil industry. Rockefeller himself remained one of the world's wealthiest individuals, having amassed a fortune that allowed him to turn his focus to philanthropy. He established institutions such as the Rockefeller Foundation, which funded medical research, education, and public health initiatives worldwide. His philanthropic efforts mirrored those of Andrew Carnegie, reflecting a broader trend among Gilded Age industrialists who sought to use their wealth for public good.

John D. Rockefeller's rise showcases the power of innovation coupled with strategic business insight, significantly reshaping the American economy. Yet, his tale also warns of the dangers inherent in unchecked corporate power, emphasizing the necessity of regulatory oversight. The rise and eventual breakup of Standard Oil underscore the complex relationship between entrepreneurial innovation, market dominance, and the regulatory frameworks shaping today's business landscape.

Reflecting on the Gilded Age, the narratives of titans like Rockefeller highlight the era's lasting influence on modern industry and economic policy. Their pioneering efforts laid the groundwork for today's industrial landscape, while their methods and the ensuing reactions shape contemporary discussions on innovation, regulation, and the dynamics of competition and monopoly. Their stories offer crucial lessons on the intricate interplay between progress and governance.

Two: Magnates and Monopolies

P icture yourself standing on Wall Street in the late 19th century, amidst the towering financial institutions that symbolize America's burgeoning economic power. The air buzzes with the frenzied energy of transactions, deals, and the constant clamor of telegraphs. This was the domain of John Pierpont Morgan, a man whose influence stretched far beyond the confines of New York City, shaping the very foundations of modern American finance. Morgan wasn't just a banker; he was a financial architect, orchestrating deals that stabilized industries and, in some cases, saved the American economy from collapse.

J.P. Morgan: Banking Titan and the Power Behind the Money

Morgan's strategic interventions in the railroad industry exemplify his prowess. During the Panic of 1893, a financial crisis that left many railroads bankrupt, Morgan stepped in with his characteristic decisiveness. He orchestrated the consolidation of several strug-gling railroads, including the New York Central and the Northern Pacific. By refinanc-ing their debts and streamlining their operations, Morgan saved these companies and stabilized the entire industry. His efforts led to the formation of vast railroad networks that crisscrossed the country, making transportation more efficient and reliable. Morgan's influence extended beyond mere financial stabilization; he set precedents for corporate governance and operational efficiency that would shape the future of the American railroad system.

Morgan's role in the establishment of U.S. Steel in 1901 is another testament to his monumental impact on American industry. Recognizing the inefficiencies and fierce competition within the steel industry, Morgan sought to create a unified entity that could dominate the market. He orchestrated the merger of several major steel companies, including Andrew Carnegie's Carnegie Steel Company, Elbert H. Gary's Federal Steel Company, and William Henry Moore's National Steel Company. The result was U.S. Steel, the world's first billion-dollar corporation, with a total capitalization of $1.4 billion. This colossal entity controlled every aspect of steel production, from raw materials to finished products, creating an integrated system that revolutionized industrial consolidation. U.S. Steel became a symbol of American industrial might, supplying crucial materials for infrastructure, the burgeoning automobile industry, and even World War I.

Beyond his financial and industrial conquests, Morgan was a significant cultural patron. His contributions to public institutions and the arts were substantial, reflecting a complex character who saw the value in cultural enrichment. Morgan donated considerable sums to museums and libraries, including the Metropolitan Museum of Art and the Morgan Library, which houses an invaluable collection of manuscripts, rare books, and art. These contributions were not mere acts of philanthropy but an extension of Morgan's vision for a cultured and educated society. His patronage helped shape the cultural landscape of New York City, turning it into a hub of art and learning. Morgan's support of the arts demonstrated that his influence extended beyond finance, touching the cultural and intellectual fabric of the nation.

Morgan's profound influence on modern banking is evident in his pivotal role in shaping the Federal Reserve. His decisive interventions during the Panic of 1907, acting as a de facto central banker, were crucial in stabilizing the banking sector. This episode underscored the necessity for a formal central bank to oversee monetary policy and ensure financial stability, leading to the Federal Reserve's creation in 1913. Morgan's actions during this crisis underscored the importance of central banking in safeguarding economic stability.

The enduring impact of Morgan's banking innovations is visible in today's financial frameworks. He championed consolidation, efficiency, and strategic action, setting enduring standards for corporate finance and governance. Morgan's legacy underlines the significant role of visionary strategy and decisive leadership in transforming the economic landscape, marking him as a pivotal figure of the Gilded Age whose influence extended beyond finance to shape American industry and culture.

Lesser-Known Industrial Leaders: The Unsung Heroes of the Gilded Age

While names like Carnegie, Rockefeller, and Morgan dominate the annals of the Gilded Age, numerous other industrial leaders made significant contributions that shaped their respective industries and left lasting impacts on American society. Take James Buchanan Duke, for instance. Born in 1856 in North Carolina, Duke was instrumental in revolutionizing the tobacco industry. By embracing machine-made cigarettes, Duke transformed tobacco from a labor-intensive crop into a mass-produced commodity. His use of automated cigarette rolling machines allowed for unprecedented production speeds, drastically lowering costs and making cigarettes affordable to the masses. Duke's aggressive marketing strategies, including offering free samples and employing iconic advertising, helped cement his product's dominance in the market. By the time of his death, the American Tobacco Company, which he founded, controlled over 90% of the cigarette market in the United States, showcasing his remarkable influence on the industry.

Another industrial leader whose contributions are often overlooked is Gustavus Swift. Born in 1839, Swift revolutionized the meatpacking industry with his innovative use of refrigerated rail cars. Before Swift, meat had to be slaughtered near where it was consumed, limiting distribution options and leading to higher prices. Swift's innovation allowed meat to be slaughtered in Chicago and then transported across the country in refrigerated rail cars, maintaining its freshness. This not only lowered costs but also expanded the reach of meat products, making them more accessible to a broader population. Swift's approach to vertical integration—controlling every aspect of production from slaughterhouses to distribution—set new standards for efficiency and quality control in the industry. His methods significantly impacted supply chain management, influencing how goods were transported and sold across various industries.

The Gilded Age was also a period of significant contributions from diverse leaders, including women and minorities who played pivotal roles, even if they received less historical recognition. One such figure was Madam C.J. Walker, born Sarah Breedlove in 1867. Walker was the first African American woman to become a self-made millionaire, thanks to her innovative haircare products for black women. She developed a line of beauty and haircare products specifically tailored to the needs of African American women, a market that had been largely ignored by mainstream manufacturers. Walker's business acumen and marketing strategies, including door-to-door sales and beauty schools to train her sales agents, created a successful business model that empowered countless women to gain financial independence. Her contributions extended beyond business; she was a prominent philanthropist and activist, supporting various causes related to education and social justice.

Technological and business innovations were at the heart of these leaders' success. Swift's refrigerated rail cars transformed the meatpacking industry and had long-term impacts on supply chain management and consumer markets. By ensuring that perishable goods could be transported over long distances without spoiling, Swift's innovation paved the way for the modern grocery industry, where fresh produce and meat are available year-round, regardless of the season. Similarly, Duke's use of automation in cigarette production set a precedent for other industries, emphasizing the importance of technological advancements in achieving economies of scale and market dominance.

These lesser-known industrial leaders also made significant contributions to their communities through philanthropy and by shaping local economies. James Buchanan Duke, for example, endowed Duke University, transforming it into one of the leading educational institutions in the country. His philanthropy extended to various other causes, including healthcare and public works, reflecting his belief in using wealth for public good. Gustavus Swift also engaged in numerous philanthropic activities, including donations to educational institutions and public health initiatives. These efforts helped improve living standards in their communities and left lasting legacies that extended beyond their business achievements.

The stories of these unsung heroes of the Gilded Age enrich our understanding of this transformative period in American history. Their innovations and contributions, though sometimes overshadowed by more famous contemporaries, were crucial in shaping industries and communities. By recognizing their achievements, we gain a more comprehensive view of the Gilded Age, appreciating the diverse figures who played significant roles in its development.

Monopolies and Moral Questions: The Ethics of Power and Control

Envision entering a market where a single vendor dominates every stall, setting high prices with limited choices. This scenario mirrors the Gilded Age's monopolistic landscape, where figures like John D. Rockefeller utilized predatory pricing to eliminate competition, only to hike prices later for substantial profits. Such strategies, though effective for amassing power, posed serious ethical dilemmas, questioning the fairness of undermining smaller businesses for personal gain and spotlighting the tension between profit motives and ethical business practices.

The public and governmental response to these monopolistic practices was far from passive. The outcry led to the introduction of legislation aimed at curbing the power of these industrial giants. The Sherman Antitrust Act of 1890 was a landmark piece of legislation designed to prevent anti-competitive practices and monopolization. Named after Senator John Sherman, the act made it illegal to engage in activities that restrained trade or commerce. Its enforcement aimed to dismantle monopolies and promote fair competition. Legal battles ensued, with significant cases like the Northern Securities Co. vs. United States setting precedents. The Supreme Court's decision to dissolve Northern Securities, a massive railroad trust, underscored the act's potency. These legal challenges were a clear message: the era of unchecked monopolistic power was under scrutiny, and the government was ready to intervene.

The debate on corporate responsibility extends beyond the Gilded Age, resonating with modern discussions about the role of corporations in society. During the Gilded Age, the concept of "corporate responsibility" was largely absent. The primary objective was profit maximization, often at the expense of ethical considerations. However, figures like Andrew Carnegie introduced a counter-narrative with their philanthropic endeavors. Carnegie's "Gospel of Wealth" posited that the affluent had a moral obligation to redistribute their wealth for the public good. This idea, though revolutionary at the time, sparked debates still relevant today: What responsibilities do corporations and wealthy individuals have towards society? The Gilded Age serves as a historical backdrop to these ongoing discussions, providing case studies of both corporate greed and altruism.

Monopolies had profound impacts on consumers and small businesses, markedly evident through the struggles of small business owners who faced overwhelming competition from larger corporations. This imbalance often resulted in limited market diversity, higher consumer prices, and fewer product choices. Companies like Standard Oil exercised control over the entire supply chain, effectively blocking new entrants and stifling innovation. As a result, economic power became concentrated among a few, distorting market dynamics and curtailing economic diversity.

Within the broader societal landscape shaped by monopolies, the labor market experienced significant repercussions. Workers in monopoly-dominated industries found themselves with little bargaining power, facing poor working conditions, low wages, and long hours. Furthermore, monopolists leveraged their economic power to influence public policy, intertwining economic dominance with political influence. This fusion solidified their control and perpetuated their monopoly power, cementing their status at the pinnacle of both industry and society.

The moral and ethical dilemmas posed by the monopolistic practices of the Gilded Age magnates are complex and multifaceted. The era serves as a powerful reminder of the need for a balanced approach to business practices, one that considers not just economic efficiency but also fairness, competition, and the broader societal impact. These lessons continue to resonate, shaping contemporary debates about corporate power, regulation, and social responsibility.

The Impact of Robber Barons on American Society

During the Gilded Age, the so-called robber barons—industry titans who accumulated vast wealth and power—were pivotal. Their endeavors catalyzed industrial expansion, connecting the nation with railroads, fueling cities with steel, and introducing groundbreaking technologies. This era witnessed burgeoning cities, job creation, and America's ascent as an industrial behemoth. Yet, the era was marked by stark economic disparities. Amidst the splendor of the wealthy elite's extravagant lifestyles, the working masses faced grueling conditions for minimal pay, highlighting the period's contrasting realities of prosperity and hardship.

The economic disparities of the Gilded Age sharply divided American society. As industrialists amassed unprecedented wealth, they showcased it through opulent lifestyles, while the working class faced dire living conditions. This widening gap between the affluent and the impoverished underscored a rigid social hierarchy, fueling tensions and paving the way for labor movements and progressive reforms. The era's stark inequalities highlighted the urgent need for systemic change, setting the stage for the social and political shifts of the early 20th century.

Culturally, the era's magnates were depicted with a mix of admiration and disdain. Media and literary works of the time offered a nuanced view of these industrial giants. Notably, "McClure's Magazine" and investigative journalist Ida Tarbell spotlighted the ruthless strategies and moral shortcomings of figures such as Rockefeller and Carnegie, particularly Tarbell's exposé on Standard Oil's monopolistic practices. These revelations stirred public demand for accountability. Conversely, the era's literature often celebrated these tycoons as epitomes of the American Dream, charting their ascent from modest origins to vast fortunes, and thus casting them in a mythic light. This complex portrayal shaped public views, casting the robber barons as both exemplars of entrepreneurial spirit and exemplifications of unchecked ambition.

The enduring influence of the Gilded Age's robber barons on American capitalism is unmistakable. Their innovative strategies and pursuit of wealth form a critical part of the American economic narrative, highlighting the complex interplay between innovation, wealth, and the necessity for regulatory oversight. These magnates initiated discussions on corporate ethics and social responsibility that are still relevant. While their philanthropic gestures, such as Carnegie's investments in libraries and education, sought to contribute positively to society, they also served to soften the harsher impacts of their industrial practices.

As you navigate the complexities of the Gilded Age, the impact of the robber barons serves as a lens through which to understand the era's broader themes. Their influence on economic development, social stratification, cultural perceptions, and the ethos of American capitalism provides a multifaceted view of a period marked by both incredible progress and significant challenges. The legacies of these industrial giants continue to shape our understanding of wealth, power, and responsibility in modern society, offering valuable insights into the ongoing dialogue about the role of business in shaping our world

Competition and Innovation: How Monopolies Spurred Technological Advancements

The fierce competition among Gilded Age corporations wasn't just a battle for market dominance; it was a catalyst for technological innovation. Imagine the oil industry, where giants like Standard Oil fought tooth and nail for supremacy. This intense rivalry pushed companies to seek out new methods to refine and transport oil more efficiently. They developed advanced drilling techniques and better refining processes, which improved production and lowered costs. Similarly, in the steel industry, the need to stay ahead of competitors led to the adoption of the Bessemer process, revolutionizing steel production by making it faster and cheaper.

Patents played a crucial role in fostering this wave of innovation. During the Gilded Age, securing a patent was not just about protecting an invention; it was a strategic move to gain a competitive edge. Patents encouraged inventors to push the boundaries of existing technologies, knowing their ideas would be legally safeguarded. This led to notable patent wars, such as the epic battles between Thomas Edison and George Westinghouse over electric power systems. Edison's direct current (DC) system clashed with Westinghouse's alternating current (AC) system, each vying to become the standard. These legal skirmishes spurred rapid advancements in electrical engineering, ultimately benefiting the public with more efficient and widespread electric power.

Strategic alliances also significantly impacted innovation, though their effects varied. Some alliances, like the one between Andrew Carnegie and Henry Clay Frick, were highly productive. Carnegie's vision combined with Frick's managerial acumen led to unprecedented growth in the steel industry. Together, they implemented new technologies and organizational practices that set industry standards. On the flip side, alliances could stifle innovation when they aimed solely at eliminating competition. For example, the formation of trusts often led to monopolistic practices that prioritized control over progress. In such cases, the focus shifted from innovation to maintaining market dominance, hindering technological advancement.

The competitive landscape of the Gilded Age catalyzed significant technological breakthroughs, notably in steel production and electrical distribution. The advancement in steel technology facilitated the construction of iconic structures such as skyscrapers and the Brooklyn Bridge, emblematic of American innovation. Meanwhile, the rivalry between Edison's power stations and Westinghouse's AC distribution system expanded the electrical grid, making electricity widely available and setting the stage for the conveniences and industries of the modern era.

Monopolies, while often criticized for their market control, inadvertently spurred some of the most significant technological advancements of the Gilded Age. The relentless drive to outdo competitors led to a culture of continuous improvement and innovation. Patents provided the legal framework to protect and incentivize inventors, ensuring a steady stream of new ideas. Strategic alliances, when focused on progress rather than control, amplified these efforts, resulting in groundbreaking technologies that reshaped industries and society.

The Gilded Age was a period of remarkable progress, driven by the dual forces of competition and innovation. The technological advancements of this era were not just milestones; they were the building blocks of modern industrial society. As we move forward to explore the social dynamics and cultural shifts of the Gilded Age, it's clear that the innovations spurred by competition continue to influence our world today. The next chapter will delve into how these technological changes impacted daily life, social structures, and cultural norms, painting a comprehensive picture of an era that laid the groundwork for the modern age.

Three: Society and Culture Influx

Imagine entering a grand ballroom in the 1880s, the air filled with the soft glow of gas lamps and the hum of genteel conversation. Men in black dress coats and white gloves escort women adorned in intricately designed gowns, their necks and wrists sparkling with jewels. This was not merely a soirée; it was a carefully orchestrated social ritual, a spectacle of etiquette and status that defined the upper echelons of Gilded Age society.

The Social Etiquette of the Gilded Age: More Than Manners

Social rituals during the Gilded Age were intricate and multifaceted, serving as both a display of wealth and a mechanism of social control. Elaborate dinner parties and debutante balls were the epitome of these rituals. Invitations for such events were sent well in advance, often engraved on fine paper, signaling the importance and exclusivity of the occasion. Guests were expected to respond immediately and dress in formal attire, adhering to strict fashion norms. Men wore dark dress coats and fitted boots, while women donned evening dresses that emphasized an hourglass figure, accessorized with gloves and jewelry. The evening would begin with a formal greeting—bowing or tipping of hats—followed by a meticulously planned sequence of events.

Once seated at the dining table, the complexity of social etiquette became even more apparent. The dinner menu typically included nine courses, starting with soup and fish, progressing through various meats and game, and concluding with dessert. Each course was paired with a specific wine, and guests were expected to try every dish. Bad manners, such as sneezing or coughing at the table, were frowned upon, and the conversation was to be kept light and pleasant, avoiding controversial topics. After dinner, men and women often separated, the men retiring to the library for cigars and brandy, while the women moved to the parlor for tea and conversation. These rituals were not mere formalities; they were a way to reinforce social hierarchies and cohesion within the elite class.

The intricate social rituals of the Gilded Age also played a crucial role in maintaining class distinctions and influencing social mobility. For those with new wealth, navigating these rituals was essential for gaining social acceptance. The established elite often viewed nouveau riche with suspicion, and proper etiquette served as a gateway to higher social circles. Conversely, a lack of understanding or adherence to these social norms could serve as a barrier, keeping new money at arm's length. Debutante balls, where young women from affluent families were formally introduced to society, were particularly significant. These events were not just about celebration but also about making advantageous social connections and potential marriage alliances. Marrying into an established family could elevate one's social status, but this required a thorough understanding of the complex social codes.

The influence of European aristocracy on American social etiquette during the Gilded Age was profound. Many American elite families looked to Europe, particularly Britain and France, for cultural cues. This transatlantic exchange of manners and lifestyles was evident in everything from fashion to the layout of grand homes. The practice of afternoon tea, for example, was adopted by American high society from their British counterparts. Similarly, the French art of fine dining, with its multiple courses and specific etiquette, was emulated in American dining rooms. This mimicry extended to social behaviors and interactions, with American elites often adopting European-style manners to assert their sophistication and cultural refinement.

Etiquette manuals and guides became indispensable tools for those aspiring to fit into high society. Books like "Etiquette in Society, in Business, in Politics, and At Home" by Emily Post provided detailed instructions on proper behavior in various social situations. These manuals were widely consumed by the middle and upper classes, who viewed them as essential for social success. They covered everything from the appropriate way to address a guest to the correct placement of utensils at a formal dinner. For many, these guides were more than just books; they were blueprints for social navigation. In an era where social missteps could have lasting repercussions, knowing the rules of etiquette was as crucial as having wealth or connections.

As you explore the social landscape of the Gilded Age, it becomes clear that etiquette was more than just a set of rules; it was a language of power and privilege. Understanding and mastering this language could open doors to new opportunities, while ignorance of it could confine one to the margins of high society. The elaborate social rituals and strict codes of conduct were both a reflection of and a response to the rapidly changing social dynamics of the time. They offered a sense of order and stability in an era marked by rapid economic growth and social upheaval, serving as a crucial element in the complex tapestry of the Gilded Age.

Art and Architecture: Reflecting the Opulence

Imagine strolling down Fifth Avenue, marveling at the grandiose mansions that rise like palaces amidst the bustling city. The architectural innovations of the Gilded Age were nothing short of spectacular, with the Beaux-Arts style reigning supreme. This architectural style, characterized by its grandeur and classical details, was inspired by the French École des Beaux-Arts. It brought a sense of European elegance to American buildings, merging opulence with functionality. The Vanderbilt Mansion, with its intricate facades and luxurious interiors, stands as a testament to this era's architectural ambition. Similarly, The Breakers in Newport, Rhode Island, commissioned by Cornelius Vanderbilt II, epitomizes the lavish lifestyle of the American elite. Designed by architect Richard Morris Hunt, The Breakers features 70 rooms adorned with imported marble, gilded woodwork, and crystal chandeliers, reflecting the sheer extravagance that defined the period.

The role of wealthy industrialists as patrons of the arts during the Gilded Age cannot be overstated. These magnates, with their immense fortunes, significantly influenced the art scene by commissioning works and establishing cultural institutions. Andrew Carnegie, for instance, built a steel empire and contributed to the cultural landscape by founding the Carnegie Hall in New York City, a venue that quickly became a hub for world-class performances. J.P. Morgan, with his vast collection of art and rare manuscripts, established the Morgan Library and Museum, ensuring that these treasures were accessible to the public. The Metropolitan Museum of Art owes much of its early growth to the donations and support from the city's wealthiest residents, who saw art patronage as a way to cement their social status while contributing to the cultural enrichment of society.

Artistic movements during the Gilded Age mirrored the rapid changes and growing complexities of urban life. Movements like the Ashcan School emerged, focusing on more realistic and sometimes stark portrayals of everyday life. Artists such as Robert Henri and John Sloan captured the gritty reality of urban existence, painting scenes of crowded streets, tenements, and working-class neighborhoods. Their works stood in contrast to the idealized images that had previously dominated American art, offering a more nuanced and critical view of society. This shift towards realism in art was a reflection of the broader societal changes, as America grappled with issues of industrialization, immigration, and social inequality. The Ashcan School's emphasis on depicting the lives of ordinary people underscored a growing awareness of the need to address these social challenges.

Art during the Gilded Age was not confined to galleries and museums; it permeated public and private life in myriad ways. Public art installations became increasingly common, with statues, fountains, and murals adorning city parks and public spaces. These installations made art accessible to a broader audience, fostering a sense of shared cultural heritage. In private residences, art became a symbol of status and refinement. Lavish homes were decorated with fine paintings, sculptures, and decorative arts, transforming living spaces into personal galleries. The Frick Collection in New York, once the private home of industrialist Henry Clay Frick, showcases the opulent integration of art into domestic life. Frick's collection of Old Master paintings, French porcelain, and 18th-century decorative arts not only reflected his personal taste but also served as a testament to the era's cultural aspirations.

Imagine walking through a home where every room is a carefully curated exhibition, each piece chosen to reflect the owner's wealth and sophistication. Art during the Gilded Age was not just about aesthetic enjoyment; it was a means of social expression and cultural engagement. The decoration of private residences with works of art was a way for the elite to display their cultural literacy and social standing. These art-filled homes often hosted social gatherings where the appreciation of art was intertwined with the intricacies of social etiquette, further reinforcing the connection between culture and class.

The Literary Voices of Mark Twain and Edith Wharton

Imagine flipping through the pages of a novel that not only entertains but also lays bare the hypocrisies and social norms of its time. Mark Twain, born Samuel Clemens, was a master of this craft. His works, such as "The Gilded Age: A Tale of Today," written with Charles Dudley Warner, and "Adventures of Huckleberry Finn," offer scathing critiques of society and politics. In "The Gilded Age," Twain satirizes the greed and corruption that characterized the era, using colorful characters and sharp wit to expose the moral decay hidden beneath the glittering surface of wealth. The story revolves around a family seeking fortune through dubious means, mirroring the real-life pursuit of wealth at any cost that defined the period.

"Adventures of Huckleberry Finn," often hailed as one of the great American novels, delves deeper into the societal issues of its time. Through the eyes of Huck, a young boy navigating the moral complexities of a racially divided society, Twain critiques the entrenched racism and moral hypocrisy of the South. Huck's journey with Jim, an escaped slave, challenges the accepted social norms and highlights the inherent contradictions in the values of freedom and equality that America professed to uphold. Twain's use of vernacular speech and vivid descriptions brings the characters to life, making their struggles and triumphs resonate with readers. His ability to blend humor with serious social commentary made his works both accessible and profoundly impactful, shaping public perceptions and sparking conversations about the need for societal change.

Edith Wharton, on the other hand, focused her literary lens on the intricacies of gender roles and class constraints within upper-class society. Born into a wealthy New York family, Wharton had an insider's perspective on the social dynamics of the elite. Her novels, such as "The Age of Innocence" and "The House of Mirth," dissect the rigid social codes and expectations that governed the lives of women and men in her time. In "The Age of Innocence," Wharton explores the tension between individual desires and societal expectations through the story of Newland Archer, a man torn between his duty to marry a suitable woman and his love for an unconventional woman. The novel's detailed portrayal of social rituals and the consequences of defying them offers a poignant critique of the constraints imposed by society.

"The House of Mirth" presents an even more scathing examination of the fate of women in the upper echelons of society. The protagonist, Lily Bart, navigates the treacherous waters of New York high society, her beauty and charm are both her greatest assets and her ultimate downfall. Wharton's nuanced portrayal of Lily's struggles highlights the limited options available to women and the harsh judgments they faced. The novel's tragic ending underscores the devastating impact of societal expectations on individual lives, prompting readers to question the fairness and humanity of such rigid social structures. Wharton's keen observations and elegant prose bring to light the often unseen pressures and sacrifices that defined the lives of women in the Gilded Age.

The impact of Twain's and Wharton's literature on public consciousness was significant. Their works did more than entertain; they provoked thought and reflection on the social and ethical issues of their time. Twain's biting satire and Wharton's incisive critiques helped shape the national dialogue on topics such as corruption, racism, and gender inequality. By presenting these issues through compelling narratives and relatable characters, they made complex social problems accessible to a broad audience. Their influence extended beyond the literary realm, contributing to a growing awareness and demand for social reforms.

The rise of literary realism during the Gilded Age was a response to the changing social and economic landscape. Realism sought to portray life as it was, rejecting the romanticized and idealized depictions of earlier literature. Writers like Twain and Wharton embraced this movement, focusing on the everyday experiences and struggles of ordinary people. This shift towards realism reflected a broader societal trend towards confronting and addressing the realities of life, rather than escaping into fantasy. The popularity of realism during this period underscored a collective desire for authenticity and truth in the face of rapid industrialization and social change.

Gender Roles and the New Woman: Shifting Paradigms

Picture bustling city streets where women, once confined to domestic roles, stride confidently in less restrictive clothing, symbolizing their newfound freedom. This emergence of the "New Woman" during the Gilded Age reflects profound shifts in economic landscapes and social attitudes. Industrialization and urbanization opened doors for women in education, employment, and politics, ushering them into professions such as teaching, nursing, and journalism. Far from mere historical footnotes, these developments marked significant challenges to the established gender norms of the era.

The suffrage movement, led by Susan B. Anthony and Elizabeth Cady Stanton, profoundly changed societal views on women's rights. Through marches, rallies, and hunger strikes, these advocates secured the 19th Amendment's ratification in 1920, granting women the right to vote. This milestone marked a significant shift towards recognizing women's political roles and spurred further efforts for gender equality, reshaping both the political scene and societal norms.

Industrialization and urbanization reshaped family dynamics and domestic life significantly. As men spent long hours in factories and offices, women increasingly managed households and nurtured children, yet the emergence of the "New Woman" marked a departure from traditional roles. Women sought careers and personal fulfillment beyond homemaking, leading to evolving marital dynamics and shared domestic responsibilities. This period saw the domestic realm transform into a more collaborative space, mirroring wider societal shifts and influencing child-rearing practices toward embracing equality and mutual respect.

The Gilded Age saw a transformative increase in women's participation in the workforce, venturing into both white-collar roles as secretaries, typists, and clerks, and into industrial labor in textiles, food processing, and beyond. This marked a significant challenge to existing stereotypes and barriers. Reactions varied widely, with progress celebrated by some and opposed by others who adhered to traditional domestic roles for women. Nevertheless, this era underscored the vital contributions of women to the economy and

ignited a gradual shift toward gender equality, setting a foundation for future advancements.

The concept of the "New Woman" encapsulated the spirit of change and progress that
defined the Gilded Age. These women were breaking free from the constraints of the past,
embracing education, careers, and political activism. They represented a new paradigm,
one where women were seen as independent, capable, and equal partners in society. The
changes in gender roles and the rise of the "New Woman" were not just about individual
empowerment; they were about transforming societal structures and norms. This period
laid the foundation for the continued evolution of women's rights and gender equality,
influencing the course of American history.

Leisure and Entertainment: From Opera Houses to Baseball Games

On a late 1800s warm summer afternoon, the air buzzed with cheering crowds and the
distinctive crack of a bat against a ball, marking the ascendancy of organized sports.
Baseball emerged as America's beloved pastime, especially after the 1876 establishment
of the National League, which elevated the game from a casual pastime to a significant
sporting spectacle. Teams such as the Chicago White Stockings and the Boston Red
Stockings drew massive crowds, transforming baseball matches into pivotal community
events. The sport's rise mirrored a broader shift in leisure pursuits, with its emphasis on
teamwork, strategy, and skill resonating deeply, uniting diverse audiences and reinforcing
baseball's role as a cornerstone of American culture.

During the Gilded Age, public entertainment venues became pivotal to urban life.
Opera houses, theaters, and vaudeville halls proliferated, showcasing varied performances
that captivated audiences nationwide. The Metropolitan Opera House, inaugurated in
1883 in New York, epitomized high culture, drawing the elite to its lavish productions
by Verdi, Wagner, and Puccini. Conversely, vaudeville theaters offered an eclectic mix
of comedy, music, and acrobatics, attracting a wider audience with affordable and diverse entertainment. This expansion of venues facilitated a democratization of the arts,
bridging social divides and making performances accessible to all, not just the affluent.

Landmark theaters like New York's Palace Theatre became cultural beacons, reflecting the Gilded Age's vibrant and varied entertainment landscape.

The landscape of music and dance underwent profound shifts, reflecting the broader societal transformations of the Gilded Age. Ragtime, with its vibrant, syncopated beats brought to life by the legendary Scott Joplin, captivated audiences far and wide, transcending social barriers. This era also witnessed the rise of social dances such as the two-step and the waltz, which became staples in dance halls and saloons, promoting a sense of unity among participants. A landmark in music history was also achieved with Thomas Edison's invention of the phonograph, a device that revolutionized how music was consumed. For the first time, families could enjoy the sounds of orchestras, operas, and popular tunes within the comfort of their own homes. This breakthrough not only made music more accessible to the masses but also played a pivotal role in shaping the musical tastes of the era.

Leisure activities during the Gilded Age played a crucial role in social integration, helping to bridge class divides and foster a sense of community. Organized sports like baseball brought people together, creating a shared experience that transcended social and economic differences. Fans from all walks of life gathered in stadiums, united by their love for the game and their support for their teams. Public entertainment venues, with their diverse offerings, provided spaces where people from different backgrounds could come together to enjoy a performance. The popularity of music and dance further blurred social boundaries, as people mingled on dance floors and in music halls, sharing in the joy of rhythm and movement.

Imagine the vibrant streets of New York City, alive with the tunes of street musicians, the laughter of theater-goers, and the enthusiastic cheers at baseball games. These moments of leisure did more than offer a break from daily life; they wove together a shared cultural identity. They bridged social gaps, inviting people into a shared cultural journey amid the rapid industrial growth and urban expansion of the Gilded Age. These activities provided pockets of joy and unity, reflecting the era's complex character by blending the excitement of discoveries with nostalgia for simpler times. The Gilded Age showcases how crucial leisure was in navigating the era's vast changes.

Four: Labor and Urban Life

I n the late 1800s, Pittsburgh thrived at the peak of industrialization. The air was thick with smoke from steel mills, a constant reminder of the city's relentless drive for production. As shifts ended, the streets filled with workers, their faces marked by the toll of labor yet radiating a determined spirit. It was a time of turmoil and transformation, as the labor movement began to take root, challenging norms and fiercely fighting for workers' rights.

The Great Strikes: Labor Movements That Shaped Industrial America

The Great Railroad Strike of 1877 was a pivotal moment in American labor history. Imagine the scene: workers at the Baltimore and Ohio (B&O) Railroad in Martinsburg, West Virginia, are fed up after a 10 percent wage cut, the second in less than a year, and decide they've had enough. The strike quickly spreads like wildfire to other cities, including Chicago and Pittsburgh. In Pittsburgh, the situation escalates into a full-blown riot, with workers clashing violently with the militia. The strike paralyzed the nation, halting over half of the freight on the country's railroads and involving more than 100,000 workers. The government responded with overwhelming force, deploying federal troops to quell the unrest. Despite its intensity, the strike accomplished little in terms of immediate labor reforms, but it set the stage for future labor movements by highlighting the deep-rooted tensions between labor and management.

The Haymarket Affair of 1886 in Chicago was another watershed event. It began as a peaceful rally supporting workers striking for an eight-hour workday. As night fell, the atmosphere grew charged, and someone threw a bomb at the police, resulting in chaos and violence. The police responded with gunfire, and by the end of the night, several police officers and civilians were dead or injured. The incident led to a highly controversial trial and the execution of four labor activists, who became martyrs in the eyes of many workers. The Haymarket Affair had a chilling effect on the labor movement, but it also galvanized workers and unions, reinforcing their resolve to fight for better conditions and rights.

The Homestead Strike of 1892 at Andrew Carnegie's Homestead Steel Works in Pennsylvania was another significant confrontation. Tensions had been simmering due to wage cuts and harsh working conditions. When the workers went on strike, Carnegie's plant manager, Henry Clay Frick, hired Pinkerton agents to break the strike, leading to a violent clash that left several dead on both sides. The strike ended when the state militia intervened, and the union was crushed. However, the Homestead Strike underscored the lengths to which industrialists would go to maintain control and the extreme measures workers were willing to take to defend their rights.

Labor unions emerged as the bedrock of the labor movement, advocating for workers' rights and better conditions. The American Federation of Labor (AFL), founded in 1886 by Samuel Gompers, focused on skilled workers and aimed to secure better wages, hours, and working conditions through collective bargaining. Unlike more radical organizations, the AFL sought to work within the existing political and economic systems, emphasizing gradual improvements rather than revolutionary change. Their strategies included organizing strikes, negotiating labor contracts, and lobbying for labor-friendly legislation. The AFL's pragmatic approach gained traction, making it one of the most influential labor organizations of the time.

The government and public response to labor strikes was often harsh and uncompromising. Local and federal authorities frequently sided with industrialists, using police and military forces to suppress strikes and maintain order. Public sentiment varied, with some viewing strikers as troublemakers disrupting economic stability, while others sympathized with their plight and supported their demands for fair treatment. The deployment of troops during the Great Railroad Strike and the violent repression of the Homestead Strike exemplify the government's willingness to use force to protect business interests.

The long-term impacts of these strikes on labor laws and worker rights were profound. The intense labor struggles of the Gilded Age highlighted the need for reform, leading to significant changes in labor legislation. The push for an eight-hour workday gained momentum, eventually becoming a standard practice. Safety regulations were introduced to address the hazardous conditions that many workers faced. The establishment of the Department of Labor in 1913 marked a significant step towards institutionalizing labor rights and ensuring federal oversight of labor issues. These reforms were hard-won victories, the result of years of struggle and sacrifice by countless workers and labor activists.

The labor movements and strikes of the Gilded Age were not just battles for better wages and working conditions; they were fights for dignity, respect, and the right to a fair and just life. The legacy of these movements is evident in the labor protections and rights we often take for granted today. The story of labor during this era is a testament to the power of collective action and the enduring quest for social justice.

The Life of a Factory Worker: Daily Grind and Aspirations

Before dawn, factory whistles pierced the still morning air, signaling the start of a grueling day for workers during the Gilded Age. Their days began early with a hurried breakfast before heading to the factory, where long hours stretched from sunrise to sunset. The work was repetitive and physically demanding—operating heavy machinery, assembling products, or handling raw materials. The deafening noise, thick dust, and smoke created a harsh, hazardous environment. Accidents were common, and minimal safety measures left workers vulnerable to injuries that could end their ability to work and support their families.

Economic constraints loomed large over these workers, dictating much of their lives. Wages were low, often barely enough to cover basic necessities like food, rent, and clothing. Many families lived paycheck to paycheck, with little to no savings to fall back on in times of illness or unemployment. The lack of job security added to their precarious existence; layoffs were frequent, especially during economic downturns. These economic pressures placed a significant strain on family life. Children often had to work to supplement the family income, and the constant worry about making ends meet took a toll on the workers' mental and physical health. Their social status was markedly different from that of the industrial magnates who owned the factories. While the magnates lived in opulent mansions and enjoyed luxurious lifestyles, the factory workers resided in modest houses or crowded tenements, struggling to provide for their families.

Despite the hardships, factory workers nurtured dreams of a better future. Education was seen as a route out of poverty, with many scrimping to afford schooling for their children. Some pursued new skills for better jobs. The story of Samuel Gompers, a cigar maker who rose to become a leading labor figure and founder of the American Federation of Labor, exemplified the potential for upward mobility. Moreover, the sense of community was strong; workers formed mutual aid societies and local clubs, providing financial help and fostering a spirit of solidarity and collective resilience.

The daily grind of a factory worker was grueling and relentless, a far cry from the glamorous lives of the industrial elite. Yet, within this struggle, there were moments of hope and resilience. The aspirations of workers for a better future, their efforts to improve their circumstances, and the communities they built in the face of adversity all contribute to a rich and complex portrait of life during the Gilded Age. The contrast between the lives of workers and magnates serves as a powerful reminder of the economic disparities that continue to shape our world today. The stories of factory workers are not just tales of hardship but also of perseverance and the enduring human spirit.

Urban Growth and Challenges: The Rise of American Cities

Imagine walking through the streets of New York City in the late 19th century. The city is alive with a cacophony of sounds: the clatter of horse-drawn carriages, the hum of streetcars, and the chatter of diverse crowds. This explosive urban growth was driven by a massive population shift from rural areas to cities, as people sought the economic opportunities provided by industrial jobs. Cities like New York, Chicago, and San Francisco swelled with new residents, transforming from modest urban centers into sprawling metropolises almost overnight. These cities were magnets for those seeking work in factories, construction, and emerging industries. With industrial jobs promising steady, albeit modest, incomes, families left behind the uncertainties of rural life for the bustling promises of urban living.

The rapid growth of cities brought with it a host of challenges, particularly in infrastructure and public services. Imagine the struggle of maintaining roads that were once built for horse-drawn carriages now bearing the weight of industrial transport and increased traffic. Sewage systems, initially designed for much smaller populations, were overwhelmed, leading to unsanitary conditions that were breeding grounds for diseases. Public transportation systems had to evolve quickly to keep up with the demand. Trolleys, cable cars, and eventually subways were introduced to move the growing urban populations efficiently. The sheer pace of growth meant that cities often played catch-up, with infrastructure development lagging behind the needs of the residents.

Urban development efforts, including zoning laws and public parks like New York City's Central Park, designed by Frederick Law Olmsted and Calvert Vaux, played vital roles in managing the growth of densely populated cities. These efforts provided structured land use and much-needed recreational spaces. Additionally, the advent of skyscrapers, propelled by advancements in steel construction and elevator technology, not only transformed city skylines but also optimized limited urban space, embodying the era's ambition and modernity.

However, the benefits of urban growth were accompanied by significant social challenges. Increased crime rates became a pressing issue as crowded living conditions and economic disparities created fertile ground for unlawful activities. Poverty was rampant, with many families living in squalid conditions in overcrowded tenements. These multi-story buildings, often poorly constructed and lacking basic amenities, housed multiple families in tiny, cramped apartments. Ethnic enclaves formed as immigrant communities settled in specific neighborhoods, maintaining their cultural traditions while navigating the challenges of assimilation. These enclaves provided a sense of community and support but also highlighted the divisions and tensions within the urban fabric.

Rapid urbanization brought with it intricate social challenges. As cities swelled, crime rates surged in densely populated and impoverished areas, where conditions were ripe for unlawful activities. Underfunded and ill-equipped, police forces found it difficult to establish order, casting a shadow of insecurity over urban life. Compounding these issues was widespread poverty, exacerbated by the living conditions in tenement housing. Notoriously squalid, these tenements were overcrowded, lacked proper ventilation, and were devoid of basic sanitation, all of which contributed to alarmingly high rates of sickness and death.

Ethnic enclaves, while offering a sense of community and cultural continuity, also underscored the challenges of integration. Immigrant groups often faced discrimination and hostility from native-born Americans, who saw them as competition for jobs and resources. These tensions sometimes erupted into violence and fueled nativist sentiments that influenced public policy and social attitudes. Despite these challenges, the resilience and determination of these communities contributed to the rich cultural tapestry of urban America, laying the groundwork for the multicultural cities we know today. The urban growth of the Gilded Age, with all its triumphs and trials, remains a defining chapter in the story of American development.

Immigration Waves: The New American Identity

In the late 1800s, millions of immigrants arrived at New York Harbor, stepping off crowded steamships into a bustling, multicultural scene. The air was thick with the scents of saltwater and humanity, and voices in multiple languages filled the docks. These immigrants, from Europe and Asia, came seeking new opportunities. Europeans, especially from Southern and Eastern Europe, fled economic hardship, political unrest, and religious persecution. Italians, Poles, and Jews arrived in large numbers, seeking work and security. Meanwhile, Chinese immigrants pursued fortune in the Gold Rush and later faced harsh conditions working on the transcontinental railroad, driven by the promise of prosperity.

Immigrants significantly impacted the American labor market and industries, filling challenging and low-paying jobs that native-born Americans avoided. They labored in factories, mines, and on railroads, enduring long hours in harsh conditions. Their work was pivotal to U.S. industrial growth, particularly in manufacturing and construction, undertaking dangerous tasks from laying railroad tracks in the West to toiling in urban sweatshops. This labor influx was instrumental in maintaining low production costs and high profits, facilitating rapid industrialization and economic expansion.

The cultural assimilation of immigrant groups was fraught with complexity and conflict. These communities, each with their distinct traditions, languages, and customs, enriched the American mosaic. Neighborhoods such as Little Italy and Chinatown became vibrant centers of immigrant life, offering newcomers a sense of belonging and support. However, their presence was often met with skepticism and hostility by native-born Americans, driven by fears of job competition and wage suppression. Such nativist attitudes sometimes led to violence and discrimination, illustrating the dual nature of the immigrant experience as one of both promise and hardship.

Legislative responses to the wave of immigration reflected these tensions. The Chinese Exclusion Act of 1882 was one of the earliest and most significant pieces of restrictive immigration legislation. This law banned Chinese laborers from entering the United States and marked the first time a specific ethnic group was targeted for exclusion. The Act was a direct response to the growing anti-Chinese sentiment among American workers who saw Chinese laborers as economic threats. Later, the National Origins Act of 1924 further restricted immigration by establishing quotas based on national origin, severely limiting the number of immigrants from Southern and Eastern Europe and virtually excluding Asians. These laws had long-term implications, shaping American immigration policy for decades and reflecting the racial and ethnic prejudices of the time.

As you walk through the streets of a Gilded Age city, you can see the lasting impact of these immigration waves. The architecture, cuisine, festivals, and daily life in these urban centers were all influenced by the diverse cultures that immigrants brought with them. The blending of traditions created a unique American identity, one that was constantly evolving and adapting. Despite the challenges and resistance they faced, immigrants played a crucial role in building the nation, contributing to its economic growth and cultural richness. Their stories of perseverance and resilience are woven into the fabric of American history, reminding us of the enduring quest for a better life that continues to drive people to the United States.

The Tenement Experience: Living Conditions and Social Reform

Imagine standing in a dim, cramped hallway of a tenement in New York City's Lower East Side, the air heavy with the scent of overcrowding. During the Gilded Age, such tenements housed urban workers and immigrants in deplorable conditions: families squeezed into tiny, poorly ventilated rooms, often several to an apartment, in buildings constructed with scant regard for safety or sanitation. Thin walls allowed the constant intrusion of neighbors' sounds, erasing any semblance of privacy. Jacob Riis, through his evocative photography, exposed these grim realities to the public, capturing images of children sleeping on bare floors, families huddled around makeshift stoves and the oppressive darkness of narrow hallways.

The severe health consequences of tenement living, marked by rampant outbreaks of tuberculosis and cholera, were exacerbated by unsanitary conditions and the absence of clean water or adequate sewage systems. This environment, where waste freely accumulated, turned streets and alleys into hotbeds of disease. Children, the most vulnerable, faced alarmingly high infant mortality rates in these densely populated areas. Public outcry spurred significant health reforms: sanitation improvements, the introduction of proper sewage systems, and stricter building regulations for tenements. Additionally, public health campaigns aimed to boost hygiene awareness and disease prevention, marking a pivotal moment in enhancing urban living standards.

Social reformers were instrumental in alleviating the harsh realities of tenement living. Among them, Jane Addams stood out for her relentless efforts to uplift the urban poor. Through Hull House in Chicago, which she founded, Addams provided essential services like childcare, education, and healthcare to the community. This initiative became a beacon for similar establishments nationwide, advocating for improved housing, labor laws, and social services. Their advocacy not only brought the urban poor's struggles to light but also set the stage for the social welfare programs we see today, underscoring the critical role of community support in driving social change.

Tenement life significantly impacted family dynamics and community bonds. Within these confined spaces, every family member contributed to household upkeep. Women juggled domestic chores and external employment, while children often worked to aid family finances. This collective hardship nurtured solidarity and resilience among residents. Strong community ties emerged as neighbors shared resources and support. Local centers and organizations offered crucial social, cultural, and aid services, reinforcing the communal fabric of urban neighborhoods.

Navigating the complexities of tenement life reveals a narrative of hardship interwoven with resilience. The squalid, overcrowded conditions challenged residents' health and well-being but also catalyzed reform efforts. Jane Addams and other social reformers spotlighted the dire need for improved housing and services, prompting pivotal public policy changes. In these constrained environments, family dynamics and community bonds were reshaped, cultivating a deep sense of solidarity and mutual support among residents. Thus, tenement life stands as a powerful testament to the resilience and determination of those striving for a better future amidst adversity.

Urbanization and industrialization brought profound changes to American society, and the next chapter will explore how these shifts influenced the broader social and cultural landscape of the Gilded Age.

Five: Political Tides and Reforms

During the Gilded Age, the political landscape was dominated by the spoils system, where political supporters were rewarded with government jobs, often regardless of their qualifications. Lavish dinners and smoky backroom gatherings were where deals were made, and patronage was the norm. Presidents and party leaders appointed loyal supporters to government positions as rewards for electoral help, prioritizing political loyalty over merit. This system bred inefficiency and corruption, resulting in a government workforce motivated more by personal gain than by public service.

The dangers of the spoils system became tragically clear with the assassination of President James Garfield in 1881. Garfield's assassin, Charles Guiteau, was a disgruntled office-seeker who believed he deserved a political appointment for his support during the election. When his demands were not met, he took drastic action, shooting Garfield in a Washington, D.C. train station. Garfield's death shocked the nation and highlighted the inherent risks and corruption of the patronage system, galvanizing public support for civil service reform. The assassination served as a wake-up call, illustrating the dire need for a more merit-based approach to government employment. It spurred a nationwide clamor for change, as people realized the extent to which the spoils system undermined the integrity and efficiency of their government.

The Pendleton Civil Service Act of 1883, championed by President Chester A. Arthur after Garfield's assassination, was a pivotal reform that initiated the shift towards merit-based public service. Establishing the Civil Service Commission to oversee competitive exams for government positions, the Act initially covered only about 10% of federal jobs. However, it set a vital precedent, ensuring that roles were filled based on qualifications rather than political connections, thus fostering a more competent and impartial government workforce.

The Pendleton Act fundamentally transformed political patronage and governance. It curtailed the spoils system, fostering a professional, efficient, and less corrupt civil service through merit-based hiring. This shift encouraged accountability and competence, significantly expanding to cover more federal jobs and setting precedents for state and local governance. By prioritizing merit over favoritism, the Act not only enhanced public service quality but also rebuilt trust in government, marking a crucial step toward a more meritocratic and fair system.

The Pendleton Act revolutionized government employment by ensuring positions were filled based on competence rather than political connections. This shift towards merit-based hiring contributed to a more efficient and reliable administration, significantly weakening the political machines' grip on appointments. The reform democratized the public service, opening doors for a broader spectrum of candidates and fostering a fairer, more transparent political system.

Reflection Section: Considering Modern Civil Service

Take a moment to reflect on how the principles of the Pendleton Civil Service Act might apply to modern governance. How do merit-based hiring practices influence the efficiency and integrity of today's public service? What parallels can you draw between the political challenges of the Gilded Age and those we face today? Consider writing your thoughts and insights in a journal or discussing them with a book club or study group. This reflection can help deepen your understanding of the ongoing relevance of civil service reform in fostering a fair and effective government.

The Populist Movement: Rise and Impact

In the late 19th century, rural towns saw farmers gathering in local halls, their faces etched with the hardships of crop failures and debt. This discontent gave rise to the Populist movement, rooted in the struggles of the agrarian sector. Farmers faced declining crop prices, high railroad transportation costs, and crushing debt, feeling marginalized and politically powerless in a system favoring big businesses and urban interests. Their frustration led to the formation of grassroots organizations like the Grange and the Farmer's

Alliance, which addressed their economic struggles and laid the groundwork for a broader political movement.

The Populist movement crystallized in 1891 with the founding of the People's Party, advocating for broad reforms to address the economic and political challenges faced by farmers. A key element of their platform was bimetallism, proposing the use of both gold and silver to back U.S. currency, aiming to inflate the money supply, thereby raising crop prices to alleviate farmers' debts. Additionally, they demanded railroad regulation to combat the excessive fees that undercut farmers' earnings and supported the direct election of Senators to diminish corruption and bolster democratic practices, challenging the then-prevalent system of appointment by state legislatures, which was marred by cronyism.

The Populist movement, though short-lived, made its mark by propelling Populist candidates into local and state offices, highlighting its agenda. A notable milestone was James B. Weaver securing over a million votes, or 8.5% of the popular vote, in the 1892 presidential election, underscoring the movement's broad appeal. Yet, challenges abounded, especially in unifying its diverse base of farmers, laborers, and other marginalized groups. The 1896 election saw the Populist Party merging with the Democrats under William Jennings Bryan, blurring its unique stance. Despite adopting Populist principles, Bryan's defeat diluted the movement's momentum, leading to its gradual decline into the early 20th century.

Though the Populist movement waned, its impact resonated through the 20th century, notably shaping the Progressive Era. Its advocacy for railroad regulation and the direct election of Senators bore fruit, with the 17th Amendment in 1913 enshrining the latter in law. The Populists' focus on the rights of farmers and workers influenced reforms targeting big business abuses and advancing social justice. While their push for bimetallism didn't prevail, it spurred ongoing debates on monetary policy. Ultimately, the Populists' emphasis on economic fairness and political integrity laid foundational principles for future efforts to create a more balanced and just society.

The Populist movement, though short-lived, was a powerful expression of the frustrations and aspirations of the rural and agrarian sectors in late 19th-century America.

Its legacy continues to resonate, reflecting the enduring struggle for economic justice and political reform in the face of entrenched interests and systemic challenges.

Major Political Figures and the Policies They Championed

Grover Cleveland, the first Democrat in the White House post-Civil War, served two non-consecutive terms, marking him as a crucial Gilded Age figure. Renowned for prioritizing principles over politics, he aimed to diminish government corruption and promoted a merit-based civil service. Notably, Cleveland fought against protective high tariffs, which, although bolstering American industries, escalated consumer prices. This battle led to the Wilson-Gorman Tariff Act of 1894, which marginally reduced tariffs but fell short of his comprehensive vision. His presidency is also distinguished by his frequent use of veto power against what he viewed as superfluous legislation, including veterans' pension bills. Cleveland's staunch fiscal conservatism and commitment to the gold standard amidst the 1890s economic depression frequently positioned him against his party and the broader public, presenting substantial political hurdles.

William McKinley's presidency, beginning in 1897, marked a period of economic growth and expansion for the United States. McKinley was a staunch advocate of high tariffs to protect American industries, a policy evident in the Dingley Tariff Act of 1897, which raised tariff rates to record levels. This protectionist approach aimed to shield American businesses from foreign competition and stimulate domestic production. McKinley also played a crucial role in the Spanish-American War of 1898, which resulted in the U.S. acquiring territories like Puerto Rico, Guam, and the Philippines, marking a significant expansion of American influence overseas. His administration's foreign policy was characterized by a shift towards imperialism, reflecting the nation's growing confidence on the global stage. McKinley's leadership during this period of economic and territorial expansion solidified his reputation as a pro-business president, but it also sparked debates about American imperialism and its moral implications.

The political landscape of the Gilded Age was not without its controversies and challenges. Cleveland faced significant public dissent during the economic depression of the 1890s, often referred to as the Panic of 1893. His unwavering commitment to the gold standard, combined with his reluctance to implement government-sponsored public works to alleviate unemployment, led to widespread discontent. Cleveland's decision to use federal troops to break the Pullman Strike of 1894 further alienated labor groups and exacerbated tensions. McKinley, on the other hand, faced criticism for his administration's handling of the newly acquired territories following the Spanish-American War. The debate over the annexation of the Philippines was particularly contentious, with anti-imperialists arguing that it contradicted American principles of self-determination and democracy. These political challenges underscored the complexities of governance during a period of rapid economic and social change.

The legacies of Cleveland and McKinley are viewed through varied lenses. Cleveland's adherence to fiscal conservatism and his efforts to reform government corruption have earned him praise for his integrity and commitment to principle. However, his handling of economic crises and labor unrest has been criticized for lacking empathy and flexibility. McKinley's legacy is marked by his role in transforming the U.S. into a global power. His protectionist economic policies and imperialist foreign strategies laid the groundwork for America's 20th-century economic and political dominance. Yet, his expansionist policies also sparked debates about the ethical dimensions of American imperialism, debates that resonate to this day. Both presidents, through their policies and leadership styles, significantly influenced the trajectory of American governance and left indelible marks on the nation's history.

Scandals and Corruption: Exposing the Underbelly of Politics

Imagine the late 19th century, a time when the air was thick with whispers of corruption and clandestine deals. The Gilded Age was rife with scandals that rocked the political landscape, none more infamous than the Crédit Mobilier scandal. This scandal unfolded in the 1860s, involving the Union Pacific Railroad and its construction company, Crédit Mobilier of America. Key figures like Congressman Oakes Ames were implicated in a scheme where they awarded themselves lucrative contracts, reaping enormous profits while impoverishing the railroad. The scandal's exposure in 1872 revealed that even Vice President Schuyler Colfax was tainted by association. The Crédit Mobilier scandal became a symbol of the rampant corruption that plagued the era, showcasing the lengths to which individuals would go to manipulate the system for personal gain.

The Whiskey Ring scandal of 1875 exposed a vast network of corruption involving government officials, distillers, and distributors who colluded to evade whiskey taxes, defrauding the federal government of millions. Orchestrated from the Midwest to Washington, D.C., the scheme involved bribing Treasury officials to ignore the tax evasion. Uncovered by Secretary of the Treasury Benjamin Bristow, the scandal resulted in over 100 indictments, including President Ulysses S. Grant's private secretary, Orville Babcock. While Grant was not implicated, the affair tarnished his administration and further diminished public trust in the government.

These scandals had a profound impact on public trust and the political climate of the time. The Crédit Mobilier and Whiskey Ring scandals, among others, exposed the deep-seated corruption within the federal government, shaking the public's faith in their leaders. The perception that government positions were for sale and that officials were easily swayed by bribes and personal interests led to widespread cynicism. This erosion of trust fueled political debates and amplified calls for reform, as citizens demanded greater transparency and accountability in government operations. The scandals highlighted the need for a more ethical and responsible approach to governance, prompting efforts to clean up the political system.

Investigative journalism emerged as a pivotal force during the Gilded Age, transforming the media landscape. Notable publications such as The New York Sun and Harper's Weekly were at the forefront, uncovering political and business corruption with thorough reporting. This era of journalism not only enlightened the public but also compelled governmental action, establishing the press as a crucial instrument of accountability and a defender of democracy by spotlighting the abuses of power.

The Gilded Age, marked by its scandals and corruption, serves as a stark reminder of the vulnerabilities within political systems. The high-profile scandals of the era exposed the dark underbelly of politics and set the stage for significant reforms that would shape the future of American governance. The interplay between corruption, public perception, media scrutiny, and reform efforts during this period highlights the ongoing struggle to maintain ethical standards in political life.

The Gold Standard Debate and Economic Policy

Imagine a bustling 19th-century marketplace where merchants transact in gold coins, the glint of the metal symbolizing stability. This was the essence of the gold standard, a monetary system where a country's currency value was directly linked to gold. Proponents argued that the gold standard provided a stable and predictable currency, essential for international trade and investment. It prevented governments from printing excessive money, which could lead to inflation. The fixed value of currency against gold meant that prices remained relatively stable over time, fostering confidence among investors and traders.

However, the gold standard had its critics. Opponents argued that it restricted economic growth by tying the money supply to the amount of gold a country possessed. During economic downturns, the inability to expand the money supply could exacerbate recessions and lead to deflation, where prices and wages fell, making debts harder to repay. Critics also pointed out that the gold standard imposed a rigid monetary policy, limiting the government's ability to respond to economic crises through monetary stimulus. This rigidity was seen as a significant drawback in a rapidly industrializing economy that needed flexibility to adapt to changing conditions.

The gold standard had significant economic impacts during the Gilded Age, marked by growth and volatility. Its stability supported long-term investment and international trade, driving economic expansion. However, its rigidity often resulted in deflation during downturns, notably during the Panic of 1893. This severe depression saw businesses shutter, unemployment spike, and prices fall sharply, underscoring the gold standard's challenges in ensuring economic stability.

The bimetallism debate, proposing gold and silver as currency backings, peaked during the Gilded Age. Advocated by the Populist and Silverite movements, bimetallism aimed to expand the money supply, potentially easing debt burdens and spurring economic growth. Farmers and debtors particularly championed this cause, hoping to boost crop prices and ease debt repayments. William Jennings Bryan's "Cross of Gold" speech in 1896 became a rallying cry for bimetallism, pitting the interests of the common folk against those upholding the gold standard.

The push for bimetallism created significant political and economic tensions. The debate pitted rural and agrarian interests against urban and industrial ones. While farmers and small business owners saw bimetallism as a way to escape economic hardship, bankers and industrialists feared it would lead to inflation and undermine financial stability. The election of 1896, where Bryan ran as the Democratic candidate with a pro-silver platform, was a turning point. Although Bryan lost to William McKinley, the debate over bimetallism underscored the deep economic divisions in American society and the challenges of finding a monetary policy that served all interests.

The resolution of the gold standard debate significantly shaped U.S. monetary policy. With the Gold Standard Act of 1900, gold became the exclusive foundation for U.S. currency, effectively ending the bimetallism debate. Yet, its limitations prompted further reforms, culminating in the establishment of the Federal Reserve in 1913. Designed to offer a more adaptable monetary system, the Federal Reserve aimed to manage the money supply and mitigate economic fluctuations, reflecting lessons from the gold standard era to ensure both stability and flexibility in U.S. monetary policy.

The gold standard debate, with its complex interplay of economic theories and political interests, shaped the trajectory of American monetary policy. It highlighted the challenges of maintaining currency stability while fostering economic growth and responding to crises. The legacy of this debate continues to influence modern economic policies and discussions about the best ways to manage a nation's currency and economy.

As we move forward, the next chapter will delve into the societal and cultural shifts that accompanied these economic changes, exploring how the Gilded Age set the stage for the Progressive Era and its transformative impact on American life.

(1) 'Boy at Turkey Knob Mine' by Lewis Hine. Was a photographer known for exposing the harsh realities of child labor in the early 1900s.

(2) Edith Wharton was a renowned American novelist known for 'The Age of Innocence'

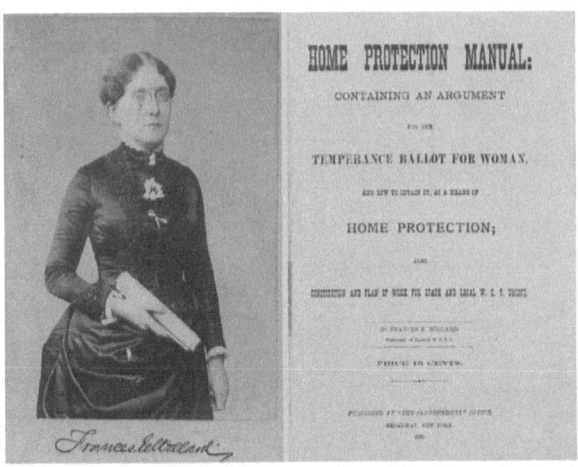

(3) Frances Willard was an American educator, a leading advocate for temperance reform, and a prominent women's suffragist.

(4) A pioneering African American journalist and activist during the Gilded Age, Ida Wells was a key figure in the anti-lynching movement and a staunch advocate for racial equality and women's rights. Photo circa 1890

(5) Photograph of the Metropolitan Museum of Art, circa 1895

(6) A scene during the rush hour while the railroad strike was in progress.

(7) Mark Twain met the celebrated European artist Teresa Feoderovna Ries in Vienna. Photo circa 1897

(8) Construction of the Brooklyn Bridge, circa 1878.

(9) Thomas Edison holding a replica of the first electric lightbulb, circa 1925

(10) Immigrant family looking for lost baggage in Ellis Island, New York. Circa 1905

(11) The construction of New York's cable car system represents a major advancement in city transit, highlighting technological innovation and improved urban mobility.

MAYOR AND COUNCILMEN OF HOBSON CITY, ALA.
YOUNG PYLES.   JESSE CUNNINGHAM.   EDW. PEARCE.
    PETER DOYLE.   S. L. DAVIS, MAYOR.   C. C. SNOW.

(12) African American influence as emerging politicians, marking early efforts toward political representation and civil rights.

(13) The renowned ballroom which doubled as an art gallery at 350 Fifth Avenue, owned by Mrs. Astor, was famous for hosting exclusive and lavish parties for 'The 400'

(14) Henry Ford with His First Model T: Ford's innovations in manufacturing, including the moving assembly line, revolutionized the auto industry during the Gilded Age.

(15) John Singer Sargent's sketches, like those for David in Saul's Camp, exemplify his contribution to art during the Gilded Age with their detailed realism and dynamic composition.

(16) Jacob Riis was a known 'muckraker' who contributed significantly to the cause of urban reform

(17) John D. Rockefeller, an oil magnate, amassed vast wealth and power by employing ruthless tactics such as bribery, intimidation, and driving competitors out of business. Despite his controversial methods, he later became a major philanthropist, donating over $500 million to education, medicine, and science.

(19) Scott Joplin was an African American composer and pianist, best known as the "King of Ragtime" for his groundbreaking contributions to the genre.

(18) Cornelius Vanderbilt began his empire with a $100 loan to run a ferry, later expanding into shipping and railroads. Known as "The Commodore," he became one of the richest men in U.S. history and shaped modern transportation.

(20) The libretto photo from Carnegie Hall's opening night on May 5, 1891, showcases the original program, featuring works conducted by Pyotr Ilyich Tchaikovsky and other notable pieces. It offers a glimpse into the historic event that marked the debut of one of the world's most iconic concert venues.

(21) Stereograph of the Vanderbilt Mansion on Fifth Avenue, circa 1850

Six: Innovations That Transformed Society

E nvision yourself in 1880s Chicago, amidst an emerging skyline reaching unprece-dented heights. The sound of construction fills the air—steel clanging, workers shouting—heralding a new era in architecture. Skyscrapers were transforming the urban landscape and redefining living and working spaces, marking a monumental shift in engineering and design.

The Advent of Skyscrapers: Architectural and Engineering Marvels

The introduction of steel-frame construction revolutionized urban skylines, enabling buildings to soar to new heights. Previously, the use of masonry restricted architectural ambitions, but steel's strength and flexibility changed the game. William Le Baron Jenney harnessed this innovation for the Home Insurance Building in Chicago, completed in 1885. Dubbed the first skyscraper, it featured a steel skeleton that supported greater height and slender designs, resilient against wind and gravity.

The use of steel was further popularized by the Bessemer process, which enabled the mass production of steel at a lower cost. This made steel economically viable for large-scale construction projects. The Chicago Fire of 1871 also played a crucial role in promoting the use of fire-resistant materials like steel, as the city sought to rebuild with more durable and safer structures. The combination of these factors paved the way for the rise of skyscrapers, changing the architectural landscape of cities worldwide.

Iconic structures such as the Woolworth Building in New York, completed in 1913, showcased the marvels of steel-frame construction. Cass Gilbert's design, with its soaring 792 feet height and neo-Gothic elegance, highlighted the aesthetic potential of steel. Similarly, Louis Sullivan, the "father of modernism," influenced skyscraper design by prioritizing form and function, as seen in the Wainwright Building in St. Louis, which featured expansive windows and open layouts, blending aesthetics with practicality in architecture.

The advent of skyscrapers had a profound impact on urban planning and real estate. The ability to build upwards rather than outwards allowed cities to accommodate growing populations and businesses within their existing footprints. This vertical expansion dramatically increased the value of urban real estate, as land in city centers became even more desirable. Skyscrapers enabled the densification of urban areas, leading to the development of central business districts where commerce and industry could thrive nearby. The rise of skyscrapers also necessitated improvements in infrastructure, such as elevators and robust utility systems, to support the increased density of people and activities.

Skyscrapers emerged as quintessential symbols of American innovation, ambition, and economic prowess, epitomizing the Gilded Age's spirit of progress. More than architectural feats, these structures stood as declarations of national pride and technological advancement. The evolving city skylines, dominated by these towering edifices, became emblems of a modern, boundless cityscape. Within popular culture, they reinforced the ideals of modernity and progress, embodying the American Dream.

The cultural significance of skyscrapers extended beyond their physical presence. They influenced art, literature, and the collective imagination, becoming metaphors for ambition and success. The construction of these architectural marvels was celebrated in newspapers and magazines, capturing the public's fascination with engineering feats and the possibilities of the future. Skyscrapers also played a role in shaping social dynamics, as they housed a mix of offices, residences, and public spaces, fostering new forms of interaction and community within the urban environment.

The rise of skyscrapers during the Gilded Age was a testament to the transformative power of technological innovation. The use of steel-frame construction revolutionized architecture, enabling the creation of buildings that reached new heights and redefined the urban experience. These towering structures became enduring symbols of progress and ambition, reflecting the spirit of an era that sought to push the boundaries of what was possible. As you marvel at the skylines of modern cities, remember that the roots of these architectural wonders lie in the pioneering efforts of the Gilded Age, a time when visionaries dared to build towards the sky.

The Automobile Revolution: From Ford's Assembly Line to Urban Impact

Imagine yourself in the early 1900s, within Henry Ford's Highland Park Plant in Michigan, where the moving assembly line was born. This innovation, introduced alongside the Model T in 1908, revolutionized manufacturing. Before this, cars were handcrafted luxuries. The assembly line's efficiency drastically cut costs and production time, making the Model T affordable and transforming personal transportation. This innovation democratized car ownership, heralding a new era of mobility for American families.

The widespread adoption of automobiles dramatically reshaped American society, granting unprecedented mobility that fueled the rise of suburbs. Freed from the need to reside near workplaces, families migrated to the suburbs, seeking more space and a quieter life away from bustling city centers. This migration spurred the decline of traditional urban areas and transformed travel, making road trips an emblem of newfound freedom. The automobile's influence extended beyond mere transportation, fostering a culture of independence and adventure that reshaped the American lifestyle.

The rapid increase in automobile ownership spurred essential changes in the nation's infrastructure. Dirt roads transformed into paved pathways, accommodating the growing number of vehicles. This development led to monumental projects like Route 66, symbolizing American wanderlust, and hastened the creation of the interstate highway system. This vast network facilitated long-distance travel and commerce, integrating the nation's economy and communities while defining road travel as a cornerstone of American identity.

Yet, the automobile's ascent introduced challenges, notably environmental. Urban pollution and congestion intensified with the proliferation of cars, their exhaust fouling the air and expansive road networks infringing upon natural terrains. Concurrently, automobile ownership reshaped American culture. The road trip became a beloved ritual, celebrated in literature and film, as families ventured across the nation. This pursuit of adventure and exploration through national parks and to distant relatives knit a tighter national fabric, enriching the American identity with shared experiences and a deeper appreciation for the country's vast landscapes and varied cultures.

Amid these changes, the automobile also transformed social interactions. Drive-in theaters became popular, offering a new way to experience movies from the comfort of one's car. The concept of the "Sunday drive" emerged, where families would take leisurely drives through the countryside, enjoying the scenery and each other's company. The car became more than just a means of transportation; it was a space for socializing, relaxation, and even romance. The design and branding of automobiles also reflected cultural trends, with sleek, stylish models symbolizing status and modernity. Car culture permeated every aspect of society, from advertising to architecture, shaping the way people lived and interacted.

As you reflect on the automobile revolution, consider its enduring legacy. The innovations introduced by Henry Ford and the subsequent societal shifts laid the groundwork for the modern world. The car remains a central part of daily life, continuing to influence urban planning, economic structures, and cultural practices. The story of the automobile revolution is a testament to the transformative power of innovation, illustrating how a single invention can reshape society in profound and lasting ways.

Breakthroughs in Medicine and Public Health

Step into a late 19th-century hospital, where the notable scent of antiseptics marks a revolutionary departure from the pervasive odors of infection and decay that once dominated. This transformation stems from groundbreaking advancements in medical technology and knowledge characteristic of the Gilded Age. Among the most pivotal was Joseph Lister's development of antiseptic procedures, using carbolic acid for sterilizing surgical instruments and wounds, significantly cutting down postoperative infections and mortality rates. This era also witnessed the refinement of surgical techniques, including William Halsted's meticulous methods and the introduction of rubber gloves, greatly reducing infection risks. These innovations saved numerous lives and established enduring surgical standards.

Public health initiatives during this period also played a crucial role in combating widespread diseases. Cities were breeding grounds for illnesses like tuberculosis and cholera, which thrived in the cramped and unsanitary conditions of urban tenements. In response, public health officials implemented comprehensive sanitation measures, including the construction of modern sewage systems and the establishment of public health departments. Vaccination programs were introduced to fight infectious diseases, with smallpox vaccination campaigns significantly reducing outbreaks. The establishment of quarantine stations for incoming immigrants helped prevent the spread of diseases from abroad. These initiatives were critical in improving urban health and reducing the incidence of deadly epidemics, making cities safer and more livable.

The Gilded Age marked a remarkable period in medical history, dramatically increasing life expectancy and fueling population growth. Before this era, short lifespans were common due to infectious diseases and surgical complications. The introduction of antiseptics and improved surgical techniques significantly lowered mortality rates, while advancements in public health, including better sanitation and widespread vaccination, made for a healthier populace. These medical breakthroughs not only saved countless lives but also reshaped labor markets and social structures, illustrating the profound impact of healthcare innovations on society.

In 1889, Johns Hopkins Hospital emerged as a beacon of medical innovation, with leaders like William Osler and William Halsted introducing residency training and blending clinical practice with medical education. This approach positioned Johns Hopkins as a pivotal entity in medical research and teaching. Concurrently, the Mayo Clinic, initiated by William Worrall Mayo and his sons, transformed healthcare by emphasizing teamwork and patient-centered care, establishing new standards in medical services. These institutions significantly advanced medical knowledge and nurtured generations of physicians committed to scientific rigor and empathetic patient care.

As you consider the advancements in medicine and public health during the Gilded Age, it becomes clear how these breakthroughs laid the foundation for modern healthcare. The development of antiseptics and improved surgical techniques revolutionized medical practice, while public health initiatives drastically reduced the spread of infectious diseases. These improvements led to increased life expectancy and population growth, shaping societal demographics in profound ways. The establishment of esteemed medical institutions further advanced medical research and education, ensuring that the gains made during this era would continue to benefit future generations. The legacy of these innovations is evident in the healthcare systems we rely on today, reflecting the enduring impact of the Gilded Age on our well-being and quality of life.

The Camera and the Dawn of Motion Pictures

Transitioning from a world where capturing an image was the domain of artists and lengthy sittings, the landscape of visual memory was transformed by George Eastman's groundbreaking innovation. Born in 1854, Eastman introduced the Kodak camera in 1888, a pivotal moment in photography's history. Before this, photography required cumbersome equipment and intricate chemical processes. The Kodak camera, however, utilized roll film and simplified photography, making it accessible to the masses. Eastman's iconic slogan, "You press the button, we do the rest," epitomized this newfound simplicity, enabling anyone to document their experiences and surroundings. This innovation democratized the field of photography, fundamentally changing how memories were captured and preserved.

The late 19th century marked the dawn of cinema, with Thomas Edison's kinetoscope introducing individuals to short films viewed through a peephole, and the Lumière brothers in France pioneering the cinématographe, a device capable of recording and projecting films to an audience. Their 1895 screening of "Arrival of a Train at La Ciotat Station" famously astounded viewers. These early cinematic experiences, capturing moments as mundane as a sneeze or as dynamic as dance, ignited the public's fascination and laid the foundational stones for the film industry's explosive growth.

Photography and cinema significantly changed the way people viewed the world. For the first time, images and scenes could be captured and shared widely, providing visual documentation of social conditions and historical events. Jacob Riis, a pioneering photojournalist, used photography to expose the harsh realities of life in New York City's tenements. His book, "How the Other Half Lives," featured stark images of overcrowded and unsanitary living conditions, sparking public outcry and calls for reform. The visual impact of his photographs brought the struggles of the poor into the public eye in a way that words alone could not. Similarly, early films offered new forms of entertainment and information. Newsreels, shown in theaters, brought moving images of current events to audiences, making distant places and happenings feel immediate and real.

The ability to capture and disseminate images had a profound impact on public opinion and early 20th-century activism. Visual media became a powerful tool for social reformers, who used photographs and films to raise awareness and garner support for their causes. The suffrage movement, for instance, utilized images of marches and rallies to highlight the determination and numbers of women fighting for the right to vote. These visual representations helped to humanize the movement and make its goals more relatable to the broader public. Photographs of child laborers, taken by Lewis Hine, were instrumental in changing labor laws. Hine's poignant images of young children working in factories and mines highlighted the need for child labor regulations and contributed to the passage of the Fair Labor Standards Act.

The cultural impact of photography and cinema extended beyond social reform. These mediums influenced art, fashion, and popular culture, shaping tastes and trends. Hollywood's rise as the center of the film industry turned actors into celebrities and set new standards for beauty and style. Movies became a communal experience, with theaters drawing diverse audiences to share in the magic of the silver screen. Photography, too, evolved as an art form, with photographers like Alfred Stieglitz pushing the boundaries of what could be achieved with a camera. Stieglitz's work, which ranged from portraits to abstract compositions, elevated photography to the status of fine art, expanding its possibilities and influence.

In this era of rapid technological advancements, the camera and motion pictures reshaped society in myriad ways. They provided new means of documenting and understanding the world, influenced public opinion and social movements, and left an indelible mark on culture and daily life.

Consumer Culture: The Rise of Advertising and Mass Marketing

Imagine walking down a bustling city street in the late 19th century, your eyes drawn to vibrant posters plastered on walls and shop windows. These advertisements, with their bold colors and catchy slogans, are not just selling products; they are selling dreams and aspirations. The rise of consumer culture during the Gilded Age saw the emergence of mass marketing techniques that forever changed the landscape of commerce. Before this era, goods were often sold in local markets or through word of mouth. But as industrial production increased, so did the need to move vast quantities of goods. Enter the world of branding, packaging, and large-scale advertising campaigns.

Branding became a powerful tool for companies looking to differentiate their products in a crowded marketplace. Soap, for example, was no longer just soap; it was "Ivory Soap," a brand that promised purity and quality. Packaging also played a crucial role, with companies investing in attractive and functional designs to catch the consumer's eye. The creation of brand identities helped build consumer loyalty, making people more likely to choose a familiar product over an unknown one. Large-scale advertising campaigns, often orchestrated by emerging advertising agencies, used newspapers, magazines, and billboards to reach a wide audience. These ads didn't just inform; they persuaded, creating a sense of need and desire for products that people might not have previously considered.

Advertising began to shape consumer behavior in profound ways. With the advent of persuasive techniques, advertisements appealed to emotions, aspirations, and social status. A housewife might be convinced to buy a particular brand of flour not because it was necessarily better, but because an ad suggested it would make her a better cook and, by extension, a better wife and mother. The narrative of advertising often played on themes of progress, modernity, and self-improvement, aligning personal success with the consumption of certain products. This shift marked the birth of the modern consumer society, where purchasing decisions were influenced as much by advertising as by necessity or quality.

Department stores and mail-order catalogs revolutionized access to a wide range of products, further fueling consumerism. Stores like Macy's in New York and Marshall

Field's in Chicago offered a shopping experience that was as much about spectacle as it was about commerce. These grand emporiums, with their lavish window displays and expansive interiors, turned shopping into an event. People came not just to buy but to experience the grandeur of the store itself. Meanwhile, mail-order catalogs from companies like Sears, Roebuck, and Co. brought the department store experience to rural America. Farmers and small-town residents could now access the same goods as their urban counterparts, delivered right to their doorstep. These catalogs offered everything from clothing to farm equipment, democratizing access to consumer goods and expanding the reach of retail.

The rise of consumer culture had a significant impact on American identity and values. It fostered a sense of materialism and economic aspiration that became central to the American Dream. The idea that anyone could attain success and happiness through hard work and consumption took hold, shaping societal values and expectations. Consumer culture also reflected and reinforced social hierarchies. The ability to purchase certain goods became a marker of status and success, creating distinctions between those who could afford the latest products and those who could not. This dynamic contributed to a consumer-driven economy where social identity was increasingly tied to material possessions.

As you think about the evolution of consumer culture, consider its lasting effects on our society. The branding, advertising, and retail innovations of the Gilded Age laid the groundwork for the consumer-driven world we live in today. The themes of materialism and economic aspiration that emerged during this period continue to influence our values and behaviors, underscoring the enduring legacy of the Gilded Age on modern American life.

The innovations and cultural shifts of the Gilded Age, from skyscrapers to advertising, have deeply influenced the fabric of modern society. As we move forward, we'll explore how these changes set the stage for the Progressive Era, where reformers sought to address the inequities and challenges brought about by rapid industrialization and urbanization.

Seven: Echoes of Change: Women and Minorities

S tep into the heart of a bustling New England textile mill in the late 19th century, where the rhythm of machinery and the aroma of cotton fill the air. Surrounded by rows of diligent women, illuminated under the soft glow of gas lamps, you witness the unsung heroines of industrial America. These workers, predominantly young and unmarried, were not just cogs in the industrial machine but pivotal figures stepping boldly out of conventional roles. The Gilded Age marked a significant era for women, as they ventured into realms of influence and initiated societal transformations that would echo through time.

Influential Women of the Gilded Age: Beyond Suffrage

Women of the Gilded Age wore many hats—industrial laborers, business owners, educators, and reformers. In the factories, women worked long hours under grueling conditions, often earning a fraction of what their male counterparts made. Yet, these industrial laborers were crucial to the nation's economic growth, producing the goods that fueled America's burgeoning industries. Away from the factories, women like Madam C.J. Walker broke barriers in business, creating empires that not only provided economic independence but also uplifted entire communities. Walker's haircare products for African American women were revolutionary, offering both beauty solutions and entrepreneurial opportunities.

The role of women in spearheading social reforms during the Gilded Age was monumental. They emerged as leaders in temperance, labor rights, and education reform, significantly influencing societal change. Figures such as Frances Willard propelled the temperance movement to reduce alcohol consumption, tying it to the broader fight for women's suffrage through the Women's Christian Temperance Union (WCTU). Similarly, advocates like Catherine Beecher promoted women's education, leading to the founding of women's colleges and expanding educational access, asserting that education empowered women to better serve as societal moral guides and informed mothers.

Prominent female figures in the Gilded Age significantly impacted American society. Ida B. Wells, an activist journalist, unveiled the horrors of lynching, igniting public and international anti-lynching movements. Her work underscored the race and gender inter-sectionality she navigated in her justice pursuits. Jane Addams co-founded Chicago's Hull House, offering social services and education to immigrants and the underprivileged, earning the Nobel Peace Prize in 1931 for her social reform efforts. Frances Willard, a leader in the temperance movement and women's suffrage advocate, showcased the influence of organized women's movements in societal transformation through her work with the Women's Christian Temperance Union.

Women also made significant contributions to culture and intellect during the Gilded Age. Edith Wharton critiqued the constraints of upper-class society on women through novels like "The Age of Innocence," highlighting the struggle between personal desires and societal expectations. Likewise, Harriet Beecher Stowe, although renowned for "Uncle Tom's Cabin," continued her advocacy for social justice, women's rights, and education during this period. Both authors used their literary talents to challenge societal norms and champion reform, extending their influence beyond the written word to become prominent advocates for social change.

Women in the Gilded Age were not just passive participants in history; they were active agents of change. Their diverse roles as laborers, business owners, educators, and reformers laid the groundwork for future generations of women to continue the fight for equality and social justice. As you explore the stories of these remarkable women, you'll see how their contributions shaped the fabric of American society and left a lasting legacy that continues to inspire and empower.

African Americans in the Gilded Age: Struggles and Triumphs

Venture into a Southern town post-Reconstruction to witness the progress reversal for African Americans. The hope of freedom and equality was overshadowed by the rise of Jim Crow laws, embedding racial discrimination and relegating African Americans to a marginalized status. Public spaces became segregated, with "colored" areas facing neglect and underfunding. Disenfranchisement tactics like literacy tests and poll taxes stripped African Americans of their voting rights, silencing their voices in the political arena. Amidst this regression, the resilience and resourcefulness of the African American community stood as a critical means of survival against the backdrop of systemic oppression.

In the face of adversity, African American leaders like Booker T. Washington and W.E .B. Du Bois emerged as pivotal figures. Washington, who founded the Tuskegee Institute in Alabama, championed vocational education and self-reliance as vehicles for African American advancement within the segregated society. His philosophy, often described as "accommodation," sought progress through education and hard work. In contrast, Du Bois, a co-founder of the NAACP and a proponent of the "Talented Tenth," advocated for direct action against racial injustices, emphasizing the need for civil rights and political representation. The differing approaches of Washington and Du Bois underscored the varied strategies within the African American community to challenge and navigate the landscape of racial inequality.

Despite the oppressive climate, African Americans made pivotal cultural contributions that laid the foundation for future movements. Music, notably the blues, rooted in spirituals and work songs, became a powerful medium to voice the struggles and hopes of African American life. Literature and the arts also saw significant contributions, with figures like Charles W. Chesnutt using their work to challenge racial stereotypes and push for social change. These cultural expressions were not merely artistic endeavors; they were acts of resilience that safeguarded African American history and identity, setting the stage for the Harlem Renaissance, which celebrated black artistic and intellectual achievement.

During the Gilded Age, African American activism thrived through grassroots efforts and strategic advocacy. Ida B. Wells, an influential journalist, led a pivotal campaign against lynching, utilizing her investigative skills to highlight racial injustices and mobilize support for anti-lynching legislation. Her work emphasized the power of media in advocating for civil rights. Simultaneously, the NAACP, with leaders like W.E.B. Du Bois, fought against racial segregation and voting disenfranchisement, securing landmark victories such as the Guinn v. United States case, which abolished disenfranchising grandfather clauses. Mutual aid societies also emerged as vital support systems for African American communities, offering financial aid, healthcare, and education to foster unity and empower individuals to advocate for their rights and improve their conditions.

The Gilded Age was a period of profound struggle and significant triumphs for African Americans. Despite the pervasive racism and systemic barriers, black leaders, institutions, and cultural contributors left an indelible mark on American society. Their efforts laid the groundwork for future civil rights movements, illustrating the enduring spirit and resilience of African-American communities.

Native American Policies and Resistance

Envision the vast American West in the late 1800s, a landscape that had been the ancestral home of Native American tribes for centuries. This era brought a seismic shift in their existence, primarily through the Dawes Act of 1887. Designed to assimilate Native Americans into American society, the federal government fragmented tribal lands into individual allotments for Native American families, fundamentally altering their communal way of life. The stark reality was devastating: over ninety million acres of tribal lands were seized and sold to non-natives, eroding cultural foundations and severing the social cohesion vital to tribal communities. This monumental land dispossession destabilized Native American economies and fragmented their societal structures, marking a profound period of upheaval.

The Dawes Act, alongside the earlier established reservation system of 1851 and the Curtis Act of 1898, systematically sought to assimilate Native Americans. The reservation system confined tribes to less fertile lands, away from their ancestral territories, to make way for European-American settlers. The Curtis Act further dismantled tribal autonomy for the "Five Civilized Tribes" (Cherokee, Chickasaw, Choctaw, Creek, and Seminole), erasing their governmental structures and legal systems. These measures aimed to disrupt tribal unity and cultural identity, marking a concerted effort to undermine Native American society.

Despite aggressive assimilation efforts, Native American leaders and communities resisted through legal battles to challenge land seizures and treaty violations. Figures like Geronimo and Sitting Bull symbolized this defiance against federal policies. Their enduring legacies inspired the preservation of Native American culture and autonomy. Tribes safeguarded their languages, traditions, and spiritual practices, with elders transmitting oral histories and cultural knowledge to younger generations, ensuring the survival of their heritage against attempts at erasure.

The resilience of Native American communities catalyzed a shift in federal policies and public attitudes towards Native American rights and sovereignty. The catastrophic consequences of the Dawes Act prompted a critical reassessment, culminating in the passage of the U.S. Indian Reorganization Act of 1934 during the Great Depression. This landmark legislation reversed the Dawes Act's land allotment system and empowered Native Americans to establish tribal governments, signifying a pivotal turn in federal policy towards honoring Native American cultural preservation and autonomy. Concurrently, advocacy by Native American leaders and the support of empathetic non-Native allies amplified awareness and acknowledgment of Native American injustices, ushering these concerns into the national dialogue.

The historical struggles of Native Americans during the Gilded Age have contemporary relevance, as many of the issues they faced continue to affect Native American communities today. Land loss and cultural erosion remain pressing concerns, with ongoing legal battles over land rights and sovereignty. The legacy of federal assimilation policies has left deep scars, contributing to social and economic challenges that persist in many Native American communities. However, the resilience and resistance demonstrated during the Gilded Age continue to inspire contemporary efforts to reclaim cultural heritage and assert tribal sovereignty. Modern movements for Native American rights, such as the protests against the Dakota Access Pipeline, draw on the same spirit of resistance that characterized the Gilded Age. These ongoing struggles underscore the long-term consequences of historical policies and the enduring fight for justice and self-determination among Native American communities.

Asian Immigrants and the Building of the West

Envision the American West in the mid-19th century, a landscape bustling with thousands of Chinese immigrants laying down tracks for the Transcontinental Railroad. With minimal equipment but immense determination, these laborers played a critical role in uniting the continent, transforming the nation's economic and geographic landscape.

The contributions of Asian immigrants, particularly Chinese laborers, to the economy and infrastructure of the Western United States were profound. By 1867, approximately 90% of the Central Pacific Railroad's workforce was Chinese. These laborers undertook some of the most perilous tasks, from blasting tunnels through the Sierra Nevada mountains to laying tracks across treacherous terrains. Their work ethic and resilience were pivotal in meeting the ambitious deadlines set by railroad companies. Leland Stanford, president of the Central Pacific and founder of Stanford University, acknowledged that completing the Transcontinental Railroad on time would have been impossible without the Chinese workers. Their contributions extended beyond the railroads, as they also engaged in various roles such as blacksmithing, carpentry, and other skilled trades, further bolstering the development of the Western U.S.

Despite their critical contributions, Asian immigrants encountered severe legal obstacles and discrimination. The Chinese Exclusion Act of 1882, a landmark in institutionalized racism, was the first federal law to ban immigration based on ethnicity, fueled by economic fears and racial prejudice against Chinese workers. This act ceased Chinese immigration and barred existing immigrants from citizenship, resulting in family separations and hindering the development of Chinese American communities. Moreover, rampant violence, segregation in housing, education, and employment, and relegation to low-wage jobs underscored the harsh social challenges they faced. This environment of exclusion and hostility profoundly affected Asian communities, leaving enduring scars and shaping their American experience for generations.

Despite adversity, Asian immigrants resiliently preserved their cultural identity while assimilating into American society. The creation of Chinatowns across the United States stands as a testament to this integration. These neighborhoods offered a refuge for preserving traditions, languages, and customs. Home to a myriad of businesses, temples, and educational institutions, Chinatowns flourished as cultural epicenters. Here, community members celebrated festivals, practiced traditional medicine, and enjoyed culinary delights, fostering a sense of belonging and solidarity in a new, often unwelcoming environment. These enclaves provided a space for cultural preservation and supported mutual aid, helping residents to navigate and thrive amidst the challenges of assimilation.

The legacy of Asian immigrants in the Gilded Age, especially Chinese laborers, is a complex narrative of substantial contributions to the American West juxtaposed against stark racial discrimination. Despite these challenges, the formation of Chinatowns and the preservation of Asian cultural heritage across the United States reflect their enduring resilience and quest for equality and acceptance in American society.

Labor Rights and Racial Integration

The bustling factories and rail yards, where the hum of machinery and the resolve of a diverse workforce marked a period of robust industrial growth in the Gilded Age. This era's labor force, a rich tapestry of cultures and races, played a crucial role in propelling America's economic ascent. Yet, beneath this surface of industrial harmony, racial tensions deeply embedded within the labor movements became apparent.

Minority labor leaders played crucial roles in advancing workers' rights and advocating for racial integration in labor unions. Among them, A. Philip Randolph stands out, who, although his prominence peaked in the early 20th century, laid the groundwork for his activism during the Gilded Age. Randolph established the Brotherhood of Sleeping Car Porters, the first labor union primarily composed of African Americans, championing improved wages and working conditions and fighting against the racial segregation prevalent in American industries. Similarly, Wong Chin Foo, a Chinese American advocate, fought tirelessly for the rights of Chinese laborers, confronting the discriminatory practices that marginalized them. These leaders were central to forging a more inclusive labor movement, connecting the fight for racial equality with labor rights.

The integration of workplaces during the Gilded Age encountered significant resistance, fueled by white workers' fears of job competition and wage impacts. This resistance was amplified by societal prejudices that influenced everyday life, relegating minority workers to the most hazardous and least desired jobs. African American workers were often confined to menial roles in the South, while skilled trades were predominantly reserved for white workers. Similarly, Chinese laborers on the Transcontinental Railroad were tasked with perilous jobs like blasting tunnels, typically receiving lower wages than their white peers. Such differential treatment perpetuated racial hierarchies within the labor force, rendering the pursuit of integration a challenging endeavor.

Despite facing numerous obstacles, significant labor actions with minority worker participation became critical milestones in advocating for labor rights and racial equality. The Great Railroad Strike of 1877, for instance, saw African American workers demanding fair wages and improved working conditions alongside their peers, showcasing unity across racial divides. Similarly, the 1892 miners' strike in Cœur d'Alene, Idaho, brought together Irish, Italian, and Slavic miners in a united front against wage cuts and unsafe working conditions, highlighting the potential for cross-ethnic solidarity in the labor movement.

The outcomes of these labor actions had far-reaching implications for labor rights and racial equality. While not all strikes achieved their immediate goals, they set important precedents for future labor movements. The inclusion of minority workers in these struggles brought attention to the intersection of race and labor, challenging the labor movement to address issues of racial discrimination within its ranks. Over time, the efforts of minority labor leaders and the solidarity displayed in these strikes contributed to the broader push for civil rights and labor reforms in the 20th century.

These stories of labor rights and racial integration during the Gilded Age illuminate the complexities of the era. They reveal how minority workers, despite facing significant obstacles, played crucial roles in shaping the labor movement. Their struggles and triumphs laid the groundwork for future generations to continue the fight for justice and equality in the workplace. The intersection of race and labor remains a critical lens through which to understand the broader social and economic dynamics of the Gilded Age.

In examining the diverse experiences of women, African Americans, Native Americans, and Asian immigrants, Chapter 7 has highlighted the multifaceted nature of the Gilded Age. Through their resilience and activism, these groups challenged the status quo and pushed for a more inclusive society. As we transition to the next chapter, we will explore the cultural and artistic renaissance that further shaped the American identity during this transformative period.

Eight: Artistic and Cultural Renaissance

Stepping into an opulent salon in the late 19th century, gilded mirrors reflect the soft glow of gas lamps, and the walls are adorned with exquisite paintings that capture the essence of the era. The room buzzes with conversation as wealthy patrons discuss the latest works by their favorite artists. This was the Gilded Age—a period of artistic flourishing and cultural transformation, where art became a mirror reflecting the societal changes and tensions of the time.

The Gilded Age in Art: Painters and Patrons

The Gilded Age saw the emergence of several prominent painters whose works left an indelible mark on American art. John Singer Sargent, a master of portraiture, captured the elegance and sophistication of high society with an almost photographic realism. His portraits, such as "Madame X" and "The Daughters of Edward Darley Boit," showcased his technical prowess and offered a window into the lives of the elite. Sargent's ability to capture the nuanced expressions and intricate details of his subjects made his work a favorite among the wealthy, who sought to immortalize themselves on canvas.

Mary Cassatt, another influential artist of the time, focused on domestic scenes and the intimate moments of women and children. Her works, like "The Child's Bath" and "Mother and Child," celebrated the tenderness and beauty of everyday life. Cassatt, who spent much of her career in France, was deeply influenced by the Impressionist movement, which is evident in her use of light and color. Her paintings not only highlighted the roles of women within the domestic sphere but also challenged traditional gender norms by presenting women as active participants in their own lives.

Winslow Homer, known for his evocative landscapes and seascapes, captured the rugged beauty of the American countryside and the lives of its people. His works, such as "Snap the Whip" and "The Gulf Stream," depicted the resilience and strength of ordinary Americans. Homer's ability to convey the raw power of nature and the human spirit made his paintings resonate with a broad audience, offering a stark contrast to the opulence of urban life.

The role of patrons in the art scene of the Gilded Age cannot be overstated. Wealthy families like the Vanderbilts and the Astors played crucial roles in the development of American art by commissioning works and supporting artists financially. These patrons saw art as a means of asserting their social status and cultural refinement. They filled their homes with masterpieces and funded public institutions like the Metropolitan Museum of Art. The Vanderbilts, for example, were known for their lavish taste in French 18th-century decorative arts, which they incorporated into their Fifth Avenue mansions with the help of decorators like Jules Allard and Joseph Duveen. This trend not only reflected their admiration for European culture but also their desire to create spaces that embodied sophistication and elegance.

The art movements and styles of the Gilded Age were as diverse as the society they reflected. American Impressionism, inspired by the French Impressionists, focused on capturing the fleeting effects of light and color. Artists like Childe Hassam and Theodore Robinson brought this style to American shores, painting vibrant scenes of urban and rural life. The Ashcan School, on the other hand, took a grittier approach, depicting the harsh realities of urban life with a raw, unfiltered lens. Artists like Robert Henri and George Bellows painted scenes of tenement buildings, crowded streets, and bustling markets, offering a stark contrast to the idyllic landscapes of their contemporaries.

Gilded Age art often provided cultural and social commentary, offering insights into the era's wealth, class, and social dynamics. Sargent's portraits, for example, subtly critiqued the superficiality and excess of high society, while Cassatt's depictions of women challenged traditional gender roles. The Ashcan School's focus on urban poverty and labor highlighted the growing divide between the rich and the poor, drawing attention to the social issues that plagued American cities. Through their works, these artists captured the complexities and tensions of the Gilded Age, providing a visual record of a society in flux.

As you explore the art of the Gilded Age, consider how these works reflect the broader societal changes and cultural transformations of the period. The paintings of Sargent, Cassatt, Homer, and others offer a window into the lives and experiences of Americans during this transformative era, capturing both the opulence and the struggles that defined the Gilded Age.

Photography and Realism: Documenting a Changing America

Venture into the bustling streets of late 19th-century New York City, with its towering buildings and vibrant daily hustle. During this era, photography underwent a revolutionary transformation, capturing urban life with unprecedented realism. The advent of portable cameras, notably George Eastman's Kodak in 1888, empowered photographers to leave their studios and immerse themselves in the streets. These more compact cameras, with quicker exposure times, allowed for spontaneous and candid captures of American life, marking a pivotal shift toward a more genuine portrayal of society.

Among the era's pivotal photographers were Jacob Riis and Lewis Hine. Riis, a Danish immigrant, illuminated the dire tenement life in New York City through his lens, notably in "How the Other Half Lives" (1890), revealing the grim living conditions of the impoverished. Using flash powder, Riis's images contrasted sharply with the era's typical portrayals of urban life. Lewis Hine similarly documented the grim realities faced by child laborers in factories and mills, his striking photographs catalyzing a push for labor reforms.

Photography, emerging as a powerful medium, captured the raw, unvarnished realities of daily life, starkly contrasting with the idealized portrayals common in paintings. This medium's authenticity transformed it into a crucial instrument for social commentary and reform. Photographers such as Riis and Hine wielded their cameras to shine a light on those often overlooked or marginalized, their powerful images articulating the struggles and resilience of their subjects more eloquently than words ever could.

The influence of photography on policy and social reform movements during the Gilded Age cannot be overstated. These visual records provided undeniable evidence of the need for change and helped to humanize the struggles of the poor and working class. They bridged the gap between the privileged and the underprivileged, making the plight of the latter more relatable and urgent to the former. The work of Riis and Hine, among others, demonstrated the power of photography not just as an art form, but as a catalyst for social change.

Music and Performance: From Classical to Ragtime

Envision an exquisite ball in the twilight of the 19th century, with the grandeur of the hall accentuated by the melodic strains of a symphony orchestra. The music, both grand and emotive, perfectly complements the lavishness and elegance of the evening. During the Gilded Age, the development of musical styles reflected significant societal shifts. Classical music remained the cultural cornerstone of the elite, deeply rooted in European traditions. Figures such as John Philip Sousa, celebrated for his rousing marches, alongside Antonín Dvořák, who wove American elements into his classical compositions, enchanted audiences with their sophisticated and deeply moving pieces.

Beyond classical symphonies, the Gilded Age was also defined by ragtime, a distinctly American music genre. Scott Joplin, the "King of Ragtime," brought fresh energy to the era with hits like "The Entertainer" and "Maple Leaf Rag." This music's syncopated beats and lively tunes appealed to a wide audience, marking a cultural shift towards more accessible and relaxed forms of entertainment. This transition reflected the era's move from Victorian formality to a more inclusive and vibrant cultural scene.

Music was pivotal in the Gilded Age's social and public spheres, transcending mere entertainment to become a marker of status and community cohesion. The elite frequented the Metropolitan Opera House, using opera as a stage for displaying cultural refinement and forging social ties. Meanwhile, music in public parks and gatherings, performed on bandstands, united diverse communities, embodying a collective cultural spirit that transcended societal boundaries.

Immigrant musicians enriched the American musical landscape of the Gilded Age, introducing Italian opera, German orchestral music, and Irish folk tunes. Their contributions went beyond preservation; they melded their traditions with American culture, influencing its evolution. Jewish klezmer intertwined with jazz, and African American spirituals and blues laid the foundations for jazz and rock and roll. This fusion of musical traditions created a diverse and vibrant sonic tapestry, emblematic of America's cultural melting pot.

The Gilded Age was a period of profound transformation in American music and performance. From the grandeur of classical symphonies to the infectious rhythms of ragtime, the era's musical evolution reflected the broader cultural shifts and societal changes. The contributions of immigrant musicians enriched the musical landscape, making it a diverse and dynamic tapestry. As music moved from the exclusive halls of the elite to the public spaces where everyone could enjoy it, it became a powerful force for social cohesion and cultural expression. The sounds of the Gilded Age continue to resonate, offering a window into a transformative period in American history.

World's Fairs and Expositions: Showcasing Innovation and Culture

Step into the grandeur of the 1893 World's Columbian Exposition in Chicago, known as the "White City" for its gleaming, neoclassical buildings. Celebrating the 400th anniversary of Columbus's voyage, the fair showcased human ingenuity and cultural exchange, featuring monumental structures by architects Daniel Burnham and Frederick Law Olmsted. Beyond its architecture, the exposition was a marvel of technology, introducing visitors to the wonders of electricity through Thomas Edison's incandescent bulbs and electric boats, offering a glimpse into a new era.

The 1901 Pan-American Exposition in Buffalo epitomized the era's technological and cultural progress. Its Electric Tower, a 391-foot beacon lit by thousands of bulbs, symbolized advancement. The fair presented cutting-edge machinery, agricultural developments, and transportation innovations, captivating visitors with X-ray machines, electric incubators, and the Ferris wheel's expansive views. More than mere entertainment, these expositions served as educational platforms, sparking attendees' imaginations.

Cultural exhibitions at these fairs showcased a dazzling array of artifacts, performances, and exhibits from around the globe. At the World's Columbian Exposition, pavilions representing over 40 countries displayed their heritage and innovations. Highlights included the Japanese pavilion, with its elegant architecture and tranquil gardens, and the German pavilion, noted for its industrial and scientific marvels. These global showcases promoted a spirit of international unity, inviting visitors to discover cultures far beyond their own. Additionally, the Midway Plaisance offered a blend of entertainment and education, from exotic belly dancers to detailed replicas of foreign villages, infusing the fair with a vibrant, carnival-like atmosphere.

World's fairs profoundly impacted host cities and the broader American culture, driving architectural innovation and shaping urban design for generations. The 1893 Chicago Exposition catalyzed the City Beautiful movement, advocating for urban beautification and grand public spaces that enhanced civic pride and the aesthetic appeal of cities nationwide. Notably, the legacy of these fairs often persisted in physical form; for example, the Field Museum of Natural History in Chicago was established using the Columbian Exposition's artifacts and exhibits.

The impact extended beyond architecture and urban planning. These expositions popularized new foods, technologies, and cultural practices. The 1893 fair introduced Americans to the Ferris wheel, Cracker Jack, and the concept of the amusement park, laying the groundwork for future entertainment industries. The Pan-American Exposition brought attention to the potential of electricity, influencing public and private investment in electrical infrastructure. These events were also critical in shaping public perceptions of technology and progress, presenting a future where innovation could solve social and economic challenges.

The legacy of these fairs is still felt today, not only in the physical remnants and museums that preserve their history but also in the continued tradition of world expositions. They set a precedent for the global showcases that followed, such as the 1964 New York World's Fair, which introduced the world to new technologies and cultural exchanges. The spirit of these expositions lives on, reminding us of a time when the world came together to celebrate human achievement and envision a brighter future.

The Rise of Museums and Cultural Institutions

Envision traversing the majestic corridors of the Metropolitan Museum of Art, where ancient marble sculptures stand sentinel beside immortal artworks, and every corner whispers tales from ages past. This bastion of culture was conceived in 1870, born from the collective ambition of affluent New Yorkers, including John Taylor Johnston and his cohort, who aspired to establish a cultural epicenter on par with Europe's esteemed museums. United by the aspiration to uplift American culture, they contributed their fortunes to create an inclusive space, democratizing art and education for the populace.

The American Museum of Natural History, established in 1869, had a similar mission but focused on the natural world. Founded by a group of prominent citizens, including Theodore Roosevelt Sr., the museum aimed to educate the public about the wonders of nature and the importance of scientific discovery. Its grand halls were filled with dinosaur skeletons, taxidermied animals, and geological specimens, each exhibit designed to spark curiosity and inspire learning.

Museums played a crucial role in education and public engagement during the Gilded Age. They were not just repositories of artifacts but vibrant centers of learning and cultural exchange. The Metropolitan Museum of Art, for instance, offered lectures, guided tours, and educational programs aimed at making art accessible to a broader audience. These initiatives were particularly important in an era when formal education was not universally available. Museums provided an alternative venue for intellectual enrichment, fostering a love of learning and an appreciation for cultural heritage.

The collections of these institutions were as varied as they were vast. The Metropolitan Museum of Art housed everything from ancient Egyptian artifacts to European masterpieces and American decorative arts, much of it donated by affluent patrons aiming to cement their legacies. Conversely, the American Museum of Natural History concentrated on natural specimens from global expeditions, mirroring the Gilded Age elite's fascination with artistic and natural wonders.

The impact of these museums on cultural preservation and scholarship was profound. By preserving artifacts and artworks, they safeguarded cultural heritage for future generations. The Metropolitan Museum of Art, for example, became a center for art historical research, providing scholars with access to its extensive collections and fostering academic inquiry. The American Museum of Natural History played a similar role in the sciences, supporting research in fields such as paleontology, anthropology, and biology. These institutions contributed to the advancement of knowledge and helped to establish standards for museum practices, influencing how collections were cataloged, displayed, and interpreted.

Museums also played a vital role in shaping public perceptions and cultural identity. They provided a space where people could encounter different cultures and historical periods, broadening their understanding of the world. Exhibitions like those featuring French 18th-century decorative arts at the Metropolitan Museum of Art offered visitors a glimpse into the opulent lifestyles of the past, while natural history exhibits showcased the beauty and diversity of the natural world. These experiences fostered a sense of connection to both the human and natural heritage, promoting cultural appreciation and environmental awareness.

As you reflect on the rise of museums and cultural institutions during the Gilded Age, consider how these spaces enriched public life and contributed to the era's intellectual and cultural dynamism. The vision and dedication of the individuals who founded these institutions left a lasting legacy, creating places where art, science, and history could be explored and celebrated. Today, museums continue to serve as vital centers of education and cultural preservation, building on the foundations laid during this transformative period.

Nine: Controversies and Critiques

O pening a newspaper at the break of the 20th century, you're captivated by a headline promising to reveal the dark secrets of America's industrial titans. The article that follows leaves nothing hidden, unveiling the corruption, exploitation, and significant human costs of unchecked capitalism. This domain was the province of the muckrakers, journalists, and writers who wielded their pens like swords, cutting through the polished exterior of wealth to reveal the grim truths of the Gilded Age.

Critiquing the Gilded Age: The Muckrakers' Role

The term "muckraker" might conjure images of someone sifting through filth, and in a way, that's precisely what these journalists and writers did. Coined by President Theodore Roosevelt in 1906, the term initially carried a somewhat negative connotation, implying that these individuals focused too much on the negative aspects of society. However, the muckrakers embraced the label, seeing it as a badge of honor. They were committed to exposing the societal issues and corruption that plagued both big business and government, and they did so with a fervor that ignited public outrage and spurred significant reforms.

Among the most notable muckrakers was Upton Sinclair, whose novel "The Jungle" offered a harrowing look at the meatpacking industry in Chicago. Sinclair's vivid and often stomach-churning descriptions of unsanitary conditions and worker exploitation shocked the nation. He intended to shed light on the plight of the workers, but the public's reaction was overwhelmingly focused on food safety. The resulting public outcry led to the passage of the Meat Inspection Act and the Pure Food and Drug Act in 1906, marking a watershed moment in consumer protection.

Ida Tarbell was another influential figure in the muckraking movement. Her meticulous investigation into the business practices of John D. Rockefeller and the Standard Oil Company was published as a series of articles in McClure's Magazine, later compiled into the book "The History of the Standard Oil Company." Tarbell's work depicted Rockefeller as a ruthless monopolist who used cutthroat tactics to eliminate competition and consolidate his empire. Her revelations were instrumental in fueling the public's demand for antitrust legislation, ultimately leading to the breakup of Standard Oil in 1911. Tarbell's investigative rigor and narrative skill made her a pioneer in the field of investigative journalism, setting a standard for future generations.

The impact of muckraking journalism on public perception and policy cannot be overstated. These writers and photographers didn't just inform the public; they galvanized it. The vividness of their descriptions and the undeniable evidence they presented forced people to confront the darker aspects of industrialization and urbanization. Their work spurred legislative changes that addressed labor rights, food safety, housing conditions, and monopolistic practices. The public's heightened awareness and growing demand for reform were key drivers behind many of the Progressive Era's most significant achievements.

However, muckraking was not without its critics. Some accused these journalists of sensationalism, arguing that their focus on scandal and corruption overshadowed the positive aspects of industrial progress. There were also concerns about bias, as muckrakers often had clear agendas and their work sometimes blurred the lines between objective reporting and advocacy. Despite these criticisms, the lasting impact of muckraking on journalism and public advocacy is undeniable. It established a tradition of investigative journalism that continues to play a crucial role in holding powerful entities accountable and advocating for social justice.

Reflection Section: Consider the Role of Modern Muckrakers

Think about the role of investigative journalism today. How do contemporary journalists carry on the legacy of muckrakers like Sinclair, Tarbell, and Riis? Reflect on a recent investigative report that had a significant impact on public policy or perception. How did it shape your understanding of the issue? What similarities do you see between the muckrakers of the Gilded Age and today's investigative journalists? Use this reflection to appreciate the ongoing importance of rigorous, fearless journalism in promoting transparency and accountability.

Environmental Impact: Industrialization and Nature

Imagine standing at the edge of a river in the late 19th century, its surface slick with oil and refuse. The water, once teeming with fish, now barely sustains any life. This was the reality for many American waterways during the Gilded Age, as rapid industrialization led to severe environmental degradation. Factories along rivers disposed of their waste directly into the water, leading to pollution that not only harmed aquatic life but also posed significant health risks to nearby communities. The unchecked growth of industries meant that little attention was paid to environmental consequences, resulting in landscapes scarred by human activity.

The effects of industrial growth were not limited to waterways. Vast forest areas were cleared to fuel the insatiable demand for timber and to make way for expanding railroads and cities. The logging industry, driven by the need for construction materials and paper, decimated ancient forests, leaving barren lands in its wake. Mining operations, particularly for coal and precious metals, transformed entire regions. The extraction processes often left the earth riddled with tunnels and pits, and the runoff from these operations polluted streams and rivers. The once pristine landscapes of the American West, rich with biodiversity and natural beauty, were forever altered.

The environmental toll of industrialization was starkly highlighted by incidents like the repeated fires on Ohio's Cuyahoga River, ignited by industrial waste. The 1969 fire, in particular, became a notorious example of environmental degradation, catalyzing public demand for reform and leading to the establishment of the Environmental Protection Agency (EPA) in 1970. Similarly, the Great Smog of London in 1952, caused by coal emissions, underscored the deadly consequences of air pollution, influencing environmental legislation globally, including the UK's Clean Air Act of 1956.

Amidst growing environmental concerns, early conservation efforts took root, spearheaded by figures like John Muir. A fervent advocate for the preservation of the American wilderness, Muir co-founded the Sierra Club in 1892, marking a pivotal moment in the conservation movement. His dedication was instrumental in establishing the nation's first national parks, including Yosemite and Sequoia, to safeguard natural beauty and biodiversity for posterity, highlighting an evolving awareness of environmental protection.

The conservation movement gained momentum with the support of political figures, most notably President Theodore Roosevelt. Roosevelt, influenced by Muir and other conservationists, established the United States Forest Service and signed into law the Antiquities Act of 1906, which allowed for the creation of national monuments. Under his administration, millions of acres of land were set aside as national forests, wildlife refuges, and parks. This marked a significant shift in federal policy, recognizing the importance of preserving natural resources and landscapes.

The environmental challenges of the Gilded Age resonate strongly with contemporary issues. The exploitation of natural resources, deforestation, and pollution that characterized the era laid the groundwork for the modern environmental movement. Today's debates about climate change, sustainable development, and conservation can trace their roots back to the early efforts of conservationists like John Muir. The establishment of national parks and protected areas set a precedent for environmental stewardship, emphasizing the need to balance industrial growth with the preservation of nature.

As you consider the environmental legacy of the Gilded Age, it's clear that the era's challenges continue to inform current discussions about ecological sustainability. The historical battles to protect natural landscapes and address industrial pollution underscore the ongoing struggle to find harmony between progress and preservation. The lessons learned from the past serve as a reminder of the importance of vigilance and advocacy in safeguarding our planet for future generations.

Economic Disparities: Wealth and Poverty Coexisting

Strolling down Fifth Avenue in New York City during the Gilded Age offered a vivid tableau of its stark economic divides. On one side stood the Vanderbilt mansions, symbols of the era's immense wealth, with their lavish exteriors and expansive gardens. A mere turn away, the scene shifted dramatically to crowded tenement districts where families lived in dire, cramped conditions. This period was marked by extreme wealth and widespread poverty living side by side, highlighting a profound economic disparity. Titans of industry like Andrew Carnegie and John D. Rockefeller amassed colossal fortunes, affording them luxuries such as palatial residences, private railcars, and extravagant social gatherings. In stark contrast, the working class and immigrants endured long hours in factories and sweatshops for minimal wages, barely enough to meet basic living needs. The gap was more than financial; it extended to access to education, healthcare, and opportunities, perpetuating a cycle of poverty for the poor while the rich enjoyed privileges that enhanced their status and influence.

Social Darwinism and laissez-faire capitalism significantly influenced societal views on wealth and poverty. Social Darwinism misapplied Darwin's natural selection theory, suggesting the wealthy were economically "fitter" than the economically disadvantaged. This rationalized vast economic disparities, arguing that aiding the poor contradicted natural order. Conversely, laissez-faire capitalism advocated for minimal economic intervention, positing that unregulated markets would self-correct and foster prosperity. These ideologies afforded the wealthy moral and intellectual defenses for their power and the existing economic system, promoting philanthropy as optional and minimizing the role of social safety nets.

Economic disparities in the Gilded Age had stark societal impacts. Poverty-stricken neighborhoods experienced higher crime rates, driven by desperation and limited opportunities. The poor suffered from inferior health outcomes due to inadequate medical access and unhealthy living conditions, leading to widespread diseases. This stark contrast to the visible opulence of the wealthy deepened a sense of hopelessness and resentment among the working class. Consequently, life expectancy was significantly lower for workers, who faced long hours, dangerous work environments, and poor diets. These inequalities fueled social tensions, prompting workers to organize for better wages and conditions, occasionally resulting in strikes and violent confrontations.

In response to the glaring economic disparities, various reforms and philanthropic efforts emerged. Some wealthy individuals, like Andrew Carnegie, felt a sense of responsibility towards society. Carnegie's "Gospel of Wealth" advocated for the rich to use their fortunes to benefit the public. He donated millions to build libraries, schools, and universities, believing that access to education was key to social mobility. John D. Rockefeller also engaged in philanthropy, funding medical research and educational institutions. However, these efforts, while significant, were often seen as insufficient to address the systemic issues underlying poverty.

On the reform front, labor movements gained momentum, pushing for changes to improve the lives of workers. Organizations like the American Federation of Labor (AFL) fought for higher wages, shorter working hours, and safer working conditions. The Progressive Era that followed saw the implementation of various laws aimed at reducing economic inequality, such as child labor laws, minimum wage regulations, and the establishment of social safety nets. These reforms were driven by the growing recognition that unchecked capitalism had created a deeply unequal society and that government intervention was necessary to ensure basic standards of living for all citizens. The tension between wealth and poverty during the Gilded Age set the stage for ongoing debates about economic justice and the role of government in regulating the economy, debates that continue to resonate in modern society.

The Temperance Movement and Social Morality

Envision strolling through a vibrant American township in the twilight years of the 19th century. Main streets are alive with the bustling ambiance of saloons, the sounds of conviviality, and laughter mingling with the clatter of glasses. It's a common tableau, one that vividly illustrates the backdrop against which the temperance movement gained momentum. Born from the era's deep-seated moral and societal concerns, this movement drew early support from religious factions and women's groups. Spearheaded by luminaries such as Frances Willard, the Women's Christian Temperance Union (WCTU) emerged as a powerful advocate for minimizing or eliminating alcohol consumption altogether. They posited alcohol as the culprit behind a host of societal ills—domestic violence, impoverishment, and moral degradation among them. For the temperance advocates, the quest for sobriety was more than a health crusade; it was a stride toward a society marked by greater virtue and order.

Religious leaders and temperance advocates highlighted the detrimental effects of alcohol on family and societal morals, arguing it caused familial neglect and numerous social issues. The temperance movement, extending beyond mere abstinence, was a campaign for societal betterment. Through lectures, pamphlets, and demonstrations, it showcased the devastating impacts of alcoholism on families to mobilize public support. This crusade for moral upliftment and self-discipline resonated with many, portraying temperance as a pathway to societal improvement.

The temperance movement's influence on American politics was profound. By the early 20th century, the movement had gained significant traction, culminating in the ratification of the 18th Amendment in 1919, which established Prohibition. This amendment made the manufacture, sale, and transportation of alcohol illegal, reflecting the temperance movement's success in shaping public policy. The Volstead Act, which provided for the enforcement of Prohibition, further solidified the federal government's commitment to eradicating alcohol from American society. The passage of Prohibition represented a significant victory for temperance advocates, who believed that the law would lead to a reduction in crime, poverty, and other social ills associated with alcohol consumption.

However, Prohibition's enactment inadvertently fueled organized crime, as the prohibition of alcohol opened a profitable avenue for bootleggers, speakeasies, and gangsters like Al Capone. The surge in the illegal alcohol trade eroded public trust in Prohibition, with law enforcement overwhelmed by widespread non-compliance. This period witnessed a paradox: the attempt to curb alcohol consumption inadvertently escalated criminal activities, leading to a disillusionment with the policy. Critics decried Prohibition as an excessive encroachment on personal freedoms, arguing that it oversimplified complex social behaviors. The mounting opposition culminated in the repeal of Prohibition in 1933 through the 21st Amendment, acknowledging its failures and signaling a shift towards a more nuanced approach to alcohol regulation.

The legacy of the temperance movement on American culture and social policies is multifaceted. While Prohibition itself was ultimately deemed a failure, the temperance movement succeeded in embedding a lasting awareness of the potential harms of alcohol. This awareness paved the way for future public health campaigns and policies aimed at regulating alcohol consumption and addressing substance abuse. The temperance movement also left an enduring impact on American attitudes toward morality and social reform. It demonstrated the power of grassroots activism and the ability of organized social movements to effect change in public policy. The movement's emphasis on moral rectitude and social responsibility continued to influence American cultural attitudes long after the repeal of Prohibition.

Religious Movements and Societal Influence

On a serene Sunday morning in a quaint American town of the Gilded Age, the peal of church bells breaks the silence, summoning the faithful to service. This era was marked by a remarkable religious diversity that mirrored the sweeping social and cultural shifts of the time. Predominant were the Protestant denominations—Methodists, Baptists, and Presbyterians—each drawing large numbers of worshippers. The period also saw a notable influx of immigrants, enriching the religious tapestry with increased Catholic and Jewish communities, each establishing their sanctuaries and cultural centers. Moreover, this time witnessed the emergence of new religious movements and sects, showcasing the dynamic evolution of spiritual thought. Despite facing considerable adversity, The Church of Jesus Christ of Latter-day Saints (Mormons) saw growth, while Mary Baker Eddy introduced Christian Science, promoting a doctrine that married spirituality with healing practices.

Religious groups were not isolated from the social issues of their time; instead, they actively engaged with and influenced contemporary debates on poverty, immigration, and social reform. Many religious organizations saw addressing social issues as part of their moral duty. Protestant churches, for instance, were deeply involved in the Social Gospel movement, which argued that Christianity should be applied to solve social problems. They established settlement houses, provided education and support to immigrants, and campaigned for labor reforms. Catholic parishes, often situated in immigrant neighborhoods, became centers of community support, offering everything from food and shelter to job placement services. Jewish synagogues played a similar role, helping to integrate Jewish immigrants into American society while preserving their cultural and religious traditions. These religious communities provided a sense of belonging and stability in a rapidly changing world, using their moral authority to advocate for a more just and compassionate society.

Significant religious figures of the Gilded Age left a lasting impact on both religious and societal perspectives. Dwight L. Moody, an evangelical preacher, attracted massive crowds with his revival meetings and passionate sermons. Moody emphasized personal conversion and moral living, but he also addressed social issues, arguing that faith should influence every aspect of life, including business and politics. His influence extended beyond the United States, as he conducted revivals in Europe and established the Moody Bible Institute in Chicago, which trained future evangelical leaders. Mary Baker Eddy, the founder of Christian Science, introduced a new religious perspective that combined spirituality with health. Her book "Science and Health with Key to the Scriptures" became a cornerstone of the Christian Science faith, advocating for prayer-based healing and challenging traditional medical practices. Eddy's teachings attracted a dedicated following and led to the establishment of the Christian Science Monitor, a newspaper that continues to operate today. These leaders, through their teachings and actions, shaped the religious landscape and influenced broader societal attitudes.

The Gilded Age also saw a rise in secularism and religious skepticism, driven by scientific advancements and philosophical movements that challenged traditional beliefs. Charles Darwin's theory of evolution, presented in "On the Origin of Species," sparked intense debates between science and religion. Many religious leaders saw Darwinism as a direct threat to the biblical account of creation and the foundational tenets of their faith. The Scopes Trial of 1925, though occurring after the Gilded Age, epitomized this conflict, highlighting the tensions between religious literalism and scientific inquiry. Additionally, the rise of higher criticism, a scholarly approach to studying the Bible, questioned the inerrancy and divine inspiration of the scriptures. Philosophers and intellectuals like Friedrich Nietzsche and Sigmund Freud further fueled skepticism, with Nietzsche famously declaring that "God is dead," and Freud suggesting that religious beliefs were rooted in psychological needs rather than divine truth. These challenges forced religious communities to grapple with their faith in new ways, leading to a range of responses from outright rejection of modern science to attempts at reconciliation and reinterpretation.

The diversity of religious expressions during the Gilded Age, coupled with the active engagement of religious groups in social issues and the influence of significant religious leaders, created a rich and complex spiritual landscape. The era's religious dynamics were further complicated by the rise of secularism and skepticism, reflecting the broader cultural and intellectual shifts of the time. As we move forward, the legacy of these religious movements and the societal influence they wielded continue to shape contemporary discussions about faith, morality, and social justice.

Ten: The Legacy and Its Modern Echoes

Envision yourself amidst the vibrant hustle of an early 1900s city square. The soundtrack of this scene blends the rhythmic clangs of horse-drawn carriages with the buzzing of electric streetcars, all set against a backdrop of lively conversations about the latest news. It was a pivotal moment in history, a bridge between the opulence and challenges of the Gilded Age and the dawn of the Progressive Era, marked by a collective push for reform and social justice. This era emerged from a growing consensus that the stark inequalities and pervasive corruption of the past needed urgent correction, leading to a shift in public sentiment toward favoring government intervention and the promotion of social equity.

From Gilded to Progressive: The Transition to a New Era

The transition from the Gilded Age to the Progressive Era was marked by a growing recognition that unchecked industrialization and laissez-faire capitalism had led to significant social and economic problems. The dramatic wealth disparities, with the richest 1% owning over half of the country's property while nearly half of the population lived in poverty, were impossible to ignore. The corporate monopolies and trusts that flourished during the Gilded Age often operated with little regard for the public good, protected by high tariffs and political corruption. Labor unrest was rampant, with workers striking not just for better wages but for basic human dignity. These conditions set the stage for a wave of reforms aimed at reining in corporate excesses and addressing social inequities.

The Progressive Era saw the introduction of significant reforms that reshaped American society. Antitrust laws were strengthened to break up monopolies and restore competitive markets. The Sherman Antitrust Act, though passed in 1890, was actively en-

forced under President Theodore Roosevelt, leading to the breakup of major corporations like Standard Oil. Labor protections were also a key focus, with new laws aimed
at improving working conditions, reducing child labor, and establishing fair wages. The
establishment of the Department of Labor in 1913 was a testament to the growing
recognition of workers' rights. Women's suffrage was another cornerstone of Progressive
reform, culminating in the passage of the 19th Amendment in 1920, which granted
women the right to vote. This was the result of decades of activism by women who had
long been at the forefront of social reform movements.

Individuals who bridged the Gilded Age and the Progressive Era played pivotal roles
in this transformative period. Theodore Roosevelt, a quintessential figure of both eras, is
perhaps the most notable. As a Gilded Age politician, Roosevelt had witnessed firsthand
the excesses and corruption that plagued the era. His presidency marked a definitive shift
towards Progressive ideals. Roosevelt's "Square Deal" policies aimed to ensure fairness
for workers, consumers, and businesses alike. He actively pursued antitrust actions, supported labor rights, and championed conservation efforts, reflecting a broader vision of
social justice and responsible governance. Figures like Jane Addams also exemplified this
transition. Addams, a social reformer and activist, founded Hull House in Chicago to
provide social services and advocate for the poor and immigrant communities. Her work
laid the groundwork for many Progressive reforms in social welfare and labor rights.

The lessons learned from the Gilded Age were heeded in various ways during the
Progressive Era, though some issues persisted. The necessity of government regulation to
curb corporate abuses became widely accepted, leading to the establishment of regulatory
bodies and legislation aimed at protecting the public interest. The Progressive Era also
saw a push towards greater democratic participation, with reforms such as direct primary
elections, initiatives, and referendums designed to give citizens more control over their
government. However, not all lessons were fully embraced. Economic inequality, though
addressed through reforms, remained a persistent issue. The tension between economic
growth and social equity continued to be a challenge, as did the balance between government intervention and market freedoms.

Reflect on the enduring impact of the Progressive Era's reforms, and consider how the
lessons from this period can inform our approach to contemporary social and economic

challenges. The transition from the Gilded Age to the Progressive Era underscores the importance of vigilance and advocacy in the pursuit of a more just and equitable society. Reflection Section: Bridging Eras of Reform

Take a moment to reflect on the key reforms of the Progressive Era and their enduring significance. Consider how these reforms addressed the excesses of the Gilded Age and laid the foundation for modern regulatory and social policies. Think about the parallels between the issues faced then and those we encounter today. How can the lessons from this period inform our current efforts to achieve social and economic justice? Write down your thoughts in a journal or discuss them with a book club or study group. This reflection can deepen your understanding of the historical context and its relevance to contemporary issues.

As you delve into this final chapter, you'll see how the legacy of the Gilded Age continues to echo through modern America. The Progressive reforms were a response to the challenges of their time, but they also laid the groundwork for future generations to build upon. The struggle for a more just and equitable society is ongoing, and the lessons from this transformative period remain as relevant as ever. Step into this rich tapestry of history, where past and present intertwine, and consider the enduring impact of the Gilded Age and Progressive Era on our contemporary world.

The Gilded Age and Modern America: Economic and Political Parallels

Envision the commanding presence of a modern corporate boardroom, reminiscent of scenes portrayed in films, where executives clad in tailored suits deliberate on decisions that ripple across millions of lives. This tableau, though squarely set in the present, traces its lineage back to the Gilded Age. It was in this epoch that industrial titans such as Andrew Carnegie and John D. Rockefeller mastered the mechanisms of monopolies and vertical integration. These tactics enabled them to wield control over entire production and distribution chains, from the procurement of raw materials to the delivery of finished goods, effectively monopolizing markets and optimizing profits. Advancing to the present, one observes the continuation of these strategies, albeit in evolved forms. Contemporary behemoths like Apple and Amazon exemplify this legacy. Their operations, spanning production to retail, ensure their supremacy in today's competitive landscapes, echoing the dominance once held by the magnates of the Gilded Age.

In the political arena, the influence of wealth on politics remains a striking parallel between the Gilded Age and today. Back then, political corruption was rampant, with industrialists like J.P. Morgan wielding immense power over government decisions. The infamous Tammany Hall machine in New York exemplified how money could buy political influence, often at the expense of the public good. Today, while the mechanisms might be more sophisticated, the underlying dynamics haven't changed much. Campaign finance has become a hotly debated issue, with super PACs and wealthy donors exerting significant influence over elections and policy decisions. The debate over economic policy, particularly the role of government oversight, also echoes the past. During the Gilded Age, laissez-faire capitalism was the prevailing ideology, advocating minimal government intervention. This hands-off approach led to unchecked corporate power and exploitation. In contemporary times, we see similar debates over deregulation, with arguments about whether less government interference would spur economic growth or lead to greater inequality and corporate malfeasance.

The technological boom of the Gilded Age can be likened to the digital revolution of the 21st century. Just as the introduction of electricity, telephones, and automobiles transformed society back then, today's innovations on the internet, artificial intelligence, and biotechnology are reshaping our world in profound ways. Imagine living in a time when the flick of a switch could banish darkness, or a telephone call could connect you instantly with someone miles away. These were revolutionary changes that altered daily life, work, and communication. Similarly, today's digital technologies have created new industries, changed how we interact, and even how we think. The rapid advancement of technology continues to drive societal change, much like it did during the Gilded Age, highlighting the cyclical nature of technological progress and its impact on society.

Current debates on income inequality, labor rights, and corporate power are deeply rooted in issues that first emerged during the Gilded Age. The gap between the rich and the poor has once again become a pressing concern, reminiscent of the vast disparities seen in the late 19th century. During the Gilded Age, the concentration of wealth in the hands of a few industrialists led to widespread social unrest and the rise of labor movements. Today, we see similar patterns, with the top 1% holding a significant portion of the world's wealth while many workers struggle to make ends meet. The gig economy, characterized by short-term contracts and freelance work, raises questions about job security and workers' rights, echoing the labor struggles of the past.

Debates over corporate power and the role of antitrust laws also harken back to the Gilded Age. The monopolistic practices of companies like Standard Oil led to the creation of antitrust laws aimed at breaking up large corporations and promoting competition. In contemporary times, tech giants like Google and Facebook face scrutiny for their market dominance, raising concerns about competition and consumer choice. The ongoing discussions about regulating these companies reflect the enduring relevance of antitrust principles established over a century ago.

One can't help but notice the cyclical patterns in American history when examining these issues. The Gilded Age and its excesses led to the Progressive Era's reforms, which sought to address the social and economic inequalities of the time. Similarly, today's debates and movements may pave the way for future reforms aimed at creating a more equitable society. The lessons from the Gilded Age remind us that unchecked corporate power and vast economic disparities can lead to social unrest and calls for change. Understanding this historical context can provide valuable insights into our current challenges and the potential paths forward.

So, as you navigate through the complexities of modern America, remember that many of the issues we face today have deep historical roots. The strategies, debates, and challenges of the Gilded Age continue to influence our economic and political landscape, reminding us of the importance of learning from the past. In doing so, we can better understand the present and work towards a more just and equitable future.

How the Gilded Age Influenced Modern American Culture and Society

Walking through any major American city, you can see the lasting impact of Gilded Age art and architecture. The Beaux-Arts style, characterized by its grandeur and classical details, continues to shape the American cultural landscape. Buildings like New York's Grand Central Terminal and the Boston Public Library are prime examples of this architectural legacy. The emphasis on symmetry, elaborate decorations, and monumental scale set a standard for public and institutional buildings that persists today. These architectural marvels were not just about aesthetics; they symbolized progress, stability, and national pride. The rise of American art institutions during this era, fueled by the patronage of wealthy industrialists, laid the foundation for the vibrant cultural scene we enjoy today. Museums like the Metropolitan Museum of Art in New York and the Art Institute of Chicago, established during the Gilded Age, continue to be cultural beacons, attracting millions of visitors each year and housing some of the world's most significant art collections.

The social norms and class perceptions crystallized during the Gilded Age still resonate in contemporary America. The concept of the "American Dream," the idea that anyone can achieve success through hard work and determination, was solidified during this period. However, the stark social stratifications that emerged also highlighted the limitations of this dream. The Gilded Age saw the rise of a nouveau riche class, whose opulent lifestyles were often contrasted with the harsh realities faced by the working poor. This dichotomy continues to influence how we perceive class and mobility today. The idea that wealth and success are signs of virtue and hard work, while poverty is often seen as a personal failing, has deep roots in this era. These perceptions shape policies, social attitudes, and even individual aspirations, reinforcing a social hierarchy that can be difficult to break.

Symbols of the Gilded Age, such as the self-made millionaire and the philanthropic tycoon, persist in American culture and media. Figures like Andrew Carnegie and John D. Rockefeller are often romanticized as embodiments of the American success story. Their rags-to-riches narratives and subsequent charitable endeavors have left an indelible mark on how Americans interpret success and wealth. In modern times, this narrative continues with tech moguls like Bill Gates and Elon Musk, who are celebrated not only for their business acumen but also for their philanthropic contributions. The image of the self-made millionaire who gives back to society remains a powerful symbol, influencing how we view wealth and responsibility. This enduring narrative shapes our cultural norms, encouraging both the pursuit of personal success and the expectation of social responsibility from those who achieve it.

The educational and philanthropic impacts of the Gilded Age are profound and long-lasting. Educational reforms during this period aimed to make education more accessible and practical. The establishment of public high schools and the expansion of higher education institutions were significant developments. Philanthropists like Andrew Carnegie played a crucial role in this transformation. Carnegie's funding of public libraries across the United States made knowledge accessible to millions, embodying his belief in the "Gospel of Wealth," which argued that the rich had a moral obligation to distribute their wealth in ways that promoted the welfare and happiness of the common man. This ethos of philanthropy has continued to influence American society, with modern-day philanthropists funding initiatives in education, healthcare, and social services. The foundations laid during the Gilded Age have created an enduring culture of giving, where private wealth is leveraged to address public needs.

Imagine attending a public high school or visiting a public library—these institutions owe much to the educational reforms and philanthropic efforts of the Gilded Age. The idea that education should be accessible to all and that private wealth should contribute to the public good remains a cornerstone of American society. The legacy of Gilded Age philanthropy is evident in the numerous foundations and charitable organizations that continue to shape social policies and community development. The impact of these endeavors extends beyond immediate benefits, fostering a culture that values education, innovation, and social responsibility.

The Gilded Age's influence on modern American culture and society is multifaceted and enduring. From the architectural marvels that define our cityscapes to the social norms and class perceptions that shape our lives, the legacy of this transformative era is everywhere. The symbols of success and philanthropy that emerged during this time continue to resonate, influencing how we view wealth, responsibility, and the American Dream. The educational reforms and philanthropic efforts of the Gilded Age have left an indelible mark, creating a society that values knowledge, innovation, and social welfare. As we navigate the complexities of contemporary life, understanding the roots of these cultural and social dynamics can provide valuable insights into our present and future.

Symphony & Scones: A Gilded Age Soirée

This extended edition feature brings you celebrated parlor, ragtime and vaudeville tunes alongside authentic recipes and classic cocktails. Cue the era's music and whip up these period treats—from Scott Joplin's syncopated riffs to Victorian scones and sparkling mint juleps. We hope these features immerse you in the glitter and glamour of 1890, letting you taste, tap and toast your way through a truly gilded soirée.

After the Ball by Charles K. Harris, 1891

> First "million-seller" sheet music hit (5 million copies) and the ballad that launched the pop-song industry.

Maple Leaf Rag by Scott Joplin, 1899

> Joplin's breakthrough syncopated ragtime piece that set the template for an entire musical craze.

The Entertainer by Scott Joplin, 1902

> Though just past 1900, its jaunty syncopation perfectly captures the Gilded-Age dance-hall spirit.

Daisy Bell (Bicycle Built for Two) by Harry Dacre, 1892

> A vaudeville favorite—later famous as the first song sung by a computer (IBM 7094 in 1961).

The Sidewalks of New York by James W. Blake & Charles B. Lawlor, 1894

> An unofficial NYC anthem that Teddy Roosevelt revived for his 1904 campaign.

Bill Bailey, Won't You Please Come Home? by Hughie Cannon, 1902

> A plaintive vaudeville tune whose sing-along chorus endures in every Americana retrospective.

My Wild Irish Rose by Chauncey Olcott, 1899

Olcott's wistful ode to home inspired generations of Irish-American parlor singers.

In the Good Old Summer Time by George Evans & Ren Shields, 1902

Sun-soaked chorus that became a seasonal staple at every Gilded-Age picnic.

A Hot Time in the Old Town Tonight by Theodore Metz & Joe Hayden, 1896

Ragtime-tinged melody that stormed minstrel shows and early nickelodeons alike.

Wait Till the Clouds Roll By by Joseph Falzone, 1895

A sentimental tear-jerker, popularized in parlors long before the phonograph.

Little Annie Rooney by Michael Nolan, 1890

Catchy chorus and jaunty piano accompaniment made it a favorite of street performers.

Silver Threads Among the Gold by Hubert P. Danks & Eben E. Rexford, 1873

A mournful ballad that became one of the century's longest-selling parlor standards.

Grandfather's Clock by Henry Clay Work, 1876

A storytelling song so beloved it gave its name to the household timepiece it describes.

The Band Played On by John F. Palmer & Charles B. Ward, 1895

Ubiquitous march-tune crossover—beloved at dances rather than parades.

The Laughing Song by George W. Johnson, 1891

One of the first recorded hits—an infectious vaudeville novelty that sold thousands of cylinders.

Softly and Tenderly by Will L. Thompson, 1880

A gentle hymn-like parlor song, often performed at family gatherings and church socials.

Funiculi, Funicula by Luigi Denza & Peppino Turco, 1880

Italian import about the new funicular railway—adopted by American parlors for its catchy refrain.

When You and I Were Young, Maggie by James A. Butterfield & George W. Johnson, 1864

A nostalgic love song that remained in steady parlour rotation for decades thereafter.

She's Too Fat for Me by Harry S. Miller, 1901

A playful music-hall number that pushed Victorian propriety just far enough to scandalize.

In the Shade of the Old Apple Tree by Lester G. Houghton & Egbert Van Alstyne, 1905
 Though published just after 1900, its wistful melody and lyrics evoked the Gilded-Age
 nostalgia for simpler times.

 Victorian Cream Scones

origin: beloved at East Coast afternoon teas, circa 1890

ingredients

- 2 cups all-purpose flour

- ¼ cup granulated sugar

- 1 tbsp baking powder

- ½ tsp salt

- 6 tbsp cold unsalted butter, cubed

- ⅔ cup heavy cream

- 1 large egg

- 1 tsp vanilla extract

- optional: zest of 1 lemon or ½ cup currants

instructions

   1. Preheat oven to 425 °F and line a baking sheet.

   2. Whisk flour, sugar, baking powder, and salt.

   3. Cut in butter until mixture resembles coarse crumbs.

   4. Beat cream, egg, vanilla (and zest/currants); stir into dry mix until just com-
      bined.

   5. Pat into a 1″-thick round, cut into 8 wedges; place on sheet.

   6. Bake 12–15 minutes until golden. Serve warm with jam and clotted cream.
      modern tweak: fold in 1 tsp chopped lavender or swap half the sugar for honey.

 Waldorf Salad à la 1896

origin: first served at New York's Waldorf Hotel in 1896

ingredients

- 2 tart apples, cored and chopped

– ½ cup celery, thinly sliced

– ¼ cup toasted walnuts, chopped

– ¼ cup mayonnaise

– 1 tsp lemon juice

– salt and pepper to taste

instructions

    1. Toss apples, celery, and walnuts in a bowl.

    2. Whisk mayo, lemon juice, salt, and pepper; fold into fruit mixture.

    3. Chill 30 minutes before serving.

       modern tweak: stir in halved grapes or replace walnuts with candied pecans.

Neapolitan Ice Cream Bombe

origin: an opulent frozen centerpiece at grand dinner parties, turn of the century

ingredients

– 1 pint each vanilla, strawberry, and chocolate ice cream, softened

– raspberry or strawberry syrup for drizzling

instructions

    1. Line a 6-cup bowl with plastic wrap.

    2. Spread vanilla ice cream in bottom third; freeze 20 minutes.

    3. Add strawberry layer; freeze 20 minutes.

    4. Top with chocolate layer; freeze 1 hour.

    5. Unmold onto platter, drizzle with syrup and garnish with mint.
       modern tweak: swap strawberry for peach sorbet and scatter toasted almonds on
       top.

Sparkling Mint Julep

origin: staple of Southern garden parties, Gilded-Age era

ingredients (per glass)

– 8 fresh mint leaves

– 1 tsp sugar

– 2 oz bourbon (or substitute ginger ale for a mocktail)

– crushed ice

– sparkling water to top

instructions

1. Muddle mint and sugar in a julep cup or glass.

2. Fill with crushed ice; pour in bourbon.

3. Top with sparkling water; stir gently and garnish with a mint sprig.
   modern tweak: swap bourbon for peach syrup and garnish with a fresh peach
   slice.

Oysters Rockefeller

origin: created in 1899 at Antoine's Restaurant in New Orleans, named for its rich
topping

ingredients

– 12 fresh oysters on the half shell

– 4 tbsp butter

– 1 cup chopped spinach (or kale)

– 2 tbsp chopped parsley

– 2 tbsp chopped green onions

– ¼ cup bread crumbs

– salt and pepper to taste

instructions

1. Preheat oven to 450 °F. Shuck oysters onto a baking sheet.

2. Melt butter in a pan; sauté spinach, parsley, and onions until wilted.

3. Stir in bread crumbs, salt, and pepper.

4. Spoon topping over each oyster; bake 5–7 minutes until bubbly.

5. Serve immediately.

modern tweak: sprinkle grated Parmesan or swap spinach for baby kale.

Tomato Aspic Mold

origin: savory gelatin salad popular at Victorian dinner tables

ingredients

– 2 cups tomato juice

– 2 tsp unflavored gelatin

– 1 tbsp Worcestershire sauce

– ¼ cup diced celery

– 2 tbsp finely chopped onion

– salt and pepper to taste

– garnish: cucumber slices, parsley sprigs

instructions

1. Sprinkle gelatin over ¼ cup cold tomato juice; let soften 5 minutes.

2. Heat remaining juice with Worcestershire; stir in gelatin until dissolved.

3. Remove from heat; stir in celery, onion, salt, and pepper.

4. Pour into a mold; chill 4 hours until firm.

5. Unmold onto platter, garnish and serve chilled.

modern tweak: use agar-agar for a vegetarian version and add diced bell peppers.

Pineapple Upside-Down Cake

origin: popular after canned pineapple became widely available, late 1890s

ingredients

– 4 tbsp butter, melted

– ¼ cup brown sugar

– 6 pineapple rings and maraschino cherries

– 1 ½ cups cake flour

– 1 cup granulated sugar

– 1 tsp baking powder

– ½ tsp salt

- 2 large eggs

- ½ cup milk

- ½ tsp vanilla extract

instructions

    1. Preheat oven to 350 °F. Brush a 9″ pan with butter and sprinkle brown sugar evenly.

    2. Arrange pineapple rings and cherries atop sugar.

    3. Whisk flour, sugar, baking powder, and salt.

    4. Beat eggs, milk, and vanilla; stir into dry ingredients until smooth.

    5. Pour batter over fruit; bake 30–35 minutes.

    6. Let rest 5 minutes, then invert onto plate.
      modern tweak: fold ¼ cup shredded coconut into batter for extra texture.

Chicken à la King

origin: created in the 1890s (exact provenance disputed), a creamy chicken and mushroom favorite

ingredients

- 2 cups cooked chicken, diced

- 1 cup sliced mushrooms

- 2 tbsp butter

- 2 tbsp flour

- 1 cup milk

- ½ cup chicken broth

- 2 tbsp sherry (optional)

- 2 tbsp chopped pimiento or red pepper

- salt and pepper to taste

- to serve: toast points, rice, or pastry shells

instructions

    1. Sauté mushrooms in butter until golden.

2. Stir in flour and cook 1 minute.

3. Gradually whisk in milk and broth; simmer until thickened.

4. Stir in chicken, sherry, pimiento, salt, and pepper; heat through.

5. Serve over toast, rice, or in pastry shells.

   modern tweak: replace sherry with dry white wine and garnish with fresh chives.

Champagne Cocktail

origin: popular high-society toast from mid-19th century onward

ingredients (per glass)

– 1 sugar cube

– 2–3 dashes Angostura bitters

– chilled champagne or sparkling wine

– lemon twist for garnish

instructions

1. Place sugar cube in a flute; saturate with bitters.

2. Fill glass with champagne.

3. Garnish with a lemon twist; serve immediately.

   modern tweak: drop in a few fresh raspberries or use elderflower liqueur in place
   of sugar.

Claret Punch

origin: adapted from British recipes, served at Gilded-Age dinner parties

ingredients

– 1 bottle red wine (claret)

– ½ cup brandy

– ¼ cup peach liqueur or brandy

– 3 tbsp powdered sugar

– grated nutmeg for garnish

– ice cubes

instructions

1. Combine wine, brandy, liqueur, and sugar in a punch bowl; stir until sugar dissolves.

2. Add ice and sprinkle with nutmeg.

3. Ladle into glasses and serve.

modern tweak: substitute port for brandy and float fresh berry halves on top.

Extra Feature

H ere are some fun facts about the Gilded Age that highlight the era's innovation, culture, and social change.

The First Skyscraper: The Home Insurance Building in Chicago, completed in 1885, is often considered the first skyscraper.

The Birth of the Department Store: Iconic department stores like Macy's and Marshall Field's emerged, transforming the shopping experience.

Teddy Bears Origin: The teddy bear was named after President Theodore Roosevelt, inspired by a hunting trip incident in 1902.

Invention of the Elevator: Advances in elevator technology made skyscrapers feasible and revolutionized urban architecture.

Gilded Age Architecture: Grand mansions like The Breakers and the Vanderbilt Mansion were inspired by European styles, showcasing immense wealth.

The Rise of Amusement Parks: Coney Island became a popular destination, featuring attractions like the Cyclone roller coaster and the first Ferris wheel.

The Rise of Vaudeville: Vaudeville became a popular form of entertainment during the Gilded Age, featuring a variety of acts like comedy, music, and dance, appealing to diverse audiences.

Invention of the Typewriter: The typewriter was patented in 1868 by Christopher Latham Sholes, revolutionizing business communication and the role of women in the workforce.

Standardized Time Zones: The expansion of the railroad system prompted the establishment of standardized time zones in 1883.

The First National Park: Yellowstone National Park was established in 1872, reflecting a growing appreciation for nature amid industrialization.

The New York City Subway: The first subway line opened in 1904, transforming urban transport and commuting.

The Great Chicago Fire: In 1871, the Great Chicago Fire devastated the city, leading to a rapid rebuilding effort that showcased innovative architectural designs.

The Electric Light: Thomas Edison's invention of the electric light bulb in the late 1870s revolutionized public spaces and private homes.

The Transcontinental Railroad: Completed in 1869, it connected the East and West coasts, facilitating trade and travel across the country.

The Rise of the Newspaper Industry: The Gilded Age saw a boom in journalism, with sensationalist stories and yellow journalism becoming popular.

The First Modern Olympics: The first modern Olympic Games were held in Athens in 1896, reflecting the Gilded Age's fascination with sports and international competition.

The Birth of the Modern Circus: The Ringling Brothers Circus gained popularity during this era, bringing entertainment to urban and rural audiences alike.

The Spread of Electric Streetcars: Electric streetcars became popular in urban areas during the Gilded Age, transforming public transportation and contributing to suburban development.

Cultural Institutions: Many institutions, like the Metropolitan Museum of Art, were established during this era, reflecting the growing importance of arts and culture.

The Panama Canal Project: The U.S. began preliminary efforts to build the Panama Canal in the late 1800s, leading to significant geopolitical changes in the following decades.

Thank You for Reading

We're honored you chose *Gilded Age Revealed* as part of your reading journey. We hope it sparked your curiosity and brought the glamour, grit, and grandeur of the era to life.

Enjoyed the book?

We'd love to hear your thoughts. Your review not only helps others discover the book, it also supports our growing community of history lovers and curious readers.

Scan the QR code to leave a quick review, drop a like, or share what you found most fascinating.

Every bit of feedback helps keep these stories alive.

Thank you for exploring the Gilded Age with us.

References

- 10 Gilded Age landmarks in New York City still standing. (n.d.). *Town & Country*. https://www.townandcountrymag.com/leisure/travel-guide/g3947 5441/gilded-age-landmarks-nyc/

- 7 Gilded Age inventions that changed the world. (n.d.). *History.com*. https://www.history.com/news/most-important-gilded-age-inventions

- African Americans in the Gilded Age: Background essay. (n.d.). https://bri-d ocs.s3.amazonaws.com/GA-005-HandoutA_fillable.pdf

- America at work | Articles and essays | Digital collections. (n.d.). https://www.loc.gov/collections/america-at-work-and-leisure-1894-to-1915/ar ticles-and-essays/america-at-work/#:~:text=The%20working%20conditions%2 0in%20factories,and%20monotonous%20work%20for%20employees.

- American literature after the Civil War. (n.d.) . https://www.easternct.edu/speichera/understanding-literary-history-all/am erican-literature-after-the-civil-war.html

- Americans in Paris, 1860–1900. (n.d.). *The Metropolitan Museum of Art*. https://www.metmuseum.org/press/exhibitions/2006/americans-in-pari s-18601900

- Andrew Carnegie's empire: Unveiling the business strategy behind a steel ti- tan's success. (n.d.). https://keeganedwards.com/andrew-carnegies-empire-un veiling-the-business-strategy-behind-a-steel-titans-success/

- The Dawes Act (Dawes Severalty Act) (article). (n.d.). *Khan Academy*. https://www.khanacademy.org/humanities/us-history/the-gilded-age/america n-west/a/the-dawes-act#:~:text=The%20objective%20of%20the%20Dawes,an d%20sold%20to%20non%2Dnatives.

- City life in the late 19th century. (n.d.). *Library of Congress*. https://www.loc.gov/classroom-materials/united-states-history-primary-sourc e-timeline/rise-of-industrial-america-1876-1900/city-life-in-late-19th-century/ #:~:text=Between%201880%20and%201900%2C%20cities,the%20two%20dec ades%20before%201900.

- Cornelius Vanderbilt | Biography, facts, & robber baron. (n.d.). *Britannica*. https://www.britannica.com/money/Cornelius-Vanderbilt-1794-1877#:~:text =He%20greatly%20expanded%20the%20New,and%20Indianapolis%3B%20an d%20other%20railroads.

- Credit Mobilier scandal | Summary, significance, & facts. (n.d.). *Britannica*. https://www.britannica.com/money/Credit-Mobilier-Scandal

- French interiors for an American Gilded Age. (n.d.). *The Decorative Arts Trust*. https://decorativeartstrust.org/french-ny-interiors-article/

- George Eastman. (n.d.). *Kodak*. https://www.kodak.com/en/company/page/g eorge-eastman-history/

- Giants of the Gilded Age. (2006, December 12). *The Christian Science Monitor*. https://www.csmonitor.com/2006/1212/p13s02-bogn.html

- Gilded Age fashion, period & definition. (n.d.). *History.com*. https://www.his tory.com/topics/19th-century/gilded-age

- Gilded Age politics (article): The patronage system. (n.d.). *Khan Academy*. https://www.khanacademy.org/humanities/us-history/the-gilded-age/gil ded-age/a/gilded-age-politics-patronage

- Great Railroad Strike of 1877 | History, facts, & significance. (n.d.). *Britannica*. https://www.britannica.com/topic/Great-Railroad-Strike-of-1877

- Grover Cleveland: Domestic affairs. (n.d.). *Miller Center*. https://millercenter.org/president/cleveland/domestic-affairs

- How 20000 Chinese immigrants made it happen. (n.d.). *History.com*. https://www.history.com/news/transcontinental-railroad-chinese-immigrants

- How Gilded Age corruption led to the Progressive Era. (n.d.). *History.com*. https://www.history.com/news/gilded-age-progressive-era-reforms

- Jacob Riis: Revealing "How the Other Half Lives". (n.d.). *Library of Congress*. https://www.loc.gov/exhibits/jacob-riis/overview.html

- Jacob Riis and Lewis Hine. (n.d.). *Kids Discover Online*. https://online.kidsdiscover.com/unit/industrial-revolution/topic/jacob-riis-and-lewis-hine/3

- Laissez-faire policies in the Gilded Age (article). (n.d.). *Khan Academy*. https://www.khanacademy.org/humanities/us-history/the-gilded-age/gilded-age/a/laissez-faire-policies-in-the-gilded-age

- Lighting a revolution: 19th-century consequences. (n.d.). *National Museum of American History*. https://americanhistory.si.edu/lighting/19thcent/consq19.htm

- Muckrakers (article) | The age of empire. (n.d.). *Khan Academy*. https://www.khanacademy.org/humanities/us-history/rise-to-world-power/age-of-empire/a/muckrakers

- The EXODUS of public health: What history can tell us. (n.d.). https://www.ncbi.nlm.nih.gov/pmc/articles/PMC2791244/

- The founding of U.S. Steel and the power of public opinion. (n.d.). *Harvard Business School*. https://www.library.hbs.edu/us-steel/exhibition/the-founding-of-u.s.-steel-and-the-power-of-public-opinion

- The Historical Impact of Steel Construction. (n.d.). *Fire Trol*. https://fire-trol.com/history-of-steel/#:~:text=Architects%20like%20William%20Le%20Baron,providing%20unprecedented%20height%20and%20stability.

- The Moving Assembly Line and the Five-Dollar Workday. (n.d.). *Ford Motor Company*. https://corporate.ford.com/articles/history/moving-assembly-line.html

- The Populists (article) | The Gilded Age. (n.d.). *Khan Academy*. https://www.khanacademy.org/humanities/us-history/the-gilded-age/gilded-age/a/the-populists

- The Progressive Era's new woman. (n.d.). *Tammayauthor.com*. https://tammayauthor.com/uncategorized/the-progressive-eras-new-woman

- The Troubles of Pollution: Environmental impact of the industrial revolution. (n.d.). *The Collector*. https://www.thecollector.com/environmental-impact-industrial-revolution-pollution/

- The World's Columbian Exposition of 1893. (n.d.). *PBS*. https://www.pbs.org/wgbh/americanexperience/features/chicago-worlds-columbian-exposition-1893/#:~:text=Visitors%20gawked%20at%20electric%20incubators,Kinetoscope%2C%20the%20first%20moving%20pictures.

- Roots of prohibition | Prohibition | Ken Burns. (n.d.). *PBS*. https://www.pbs.org/kenburns/prohibition/roots-of-prohibition

- Sherman Antitrust Act - History, sanctions, impact. (n.d.). *Corporate Finance Institute*. https://corporatefinanceinstitute.com/resources/economics/sherman-antitrust-act/

- Social etiquette of the Gilded Age - Suzie Geisler. (n.d.). *Prezi*. https://prezi.com/k-nyhctpis46/social-etiquette-of-the-gilded-age/

- Square Deal | Definition, history, & facts. (n.d.). *Britannica*. https://www.bri

tannica.com/event/Square-Deal

- Standard Oil | History, monopoly, & breakup. (n.d.). *Britannica.* https://www.britannica.com/money/Standard-Oil#:~:text=Standard%20Oil% 20(in%20full%2C%20Standard,transportation%20in%20the%20United%20St ates.

- Wealth and poverty in the Gilded Age. (n.d.). *Gilder Lehrman Institute of American History.* https://www.gilderlehrman.org/sites/default/files/GLI_G ildedAge_sm.pdf

- Women in the Gilded Age: Two authors' insights. (n.d.). *American Ances-tors.* https://www.americanancestors.org/video-library/women-gilded-age-tw o-authors-insights

IMAGE CITATION

(1) Hine, Lewis. *Boy at Turkey Knob Mine.* circa 1908. Photograph. Library of Congress, Prints and Photographs Division.
"Child Labour." *Encyclopaedia Britannica,* Encyclopaedia Britannica, Inc., https://www.britannica.com/topic/child-labour.

(2) Wharton, Edith. *Photograph.* Encyclopaedia Britannica, Encyclopaedia Britannica, Inc., https://www.britannica.com/biography/Edith-Wharton.

(3) "On the Road to Women's Suffrage: The Home Protec-tion Ballot." *Suffrage 2020 Illinois,* 24 Jan. 2020, https://suffrage2020illi-nois.org/2020/01/24/on-the-road-to-womens-suffrage-the-home-protection-ballot/.

(4) Schomburg Center for Research in Black Culture, Photographs and Prints Division, The New York Public Library. "Ida B. Wells-Barnett, journalist and civil rights activist" *The New York Public Library Digital Collections*. 1890 - 1910. https://digitalcollections.nypl.org/items/8694185c-b326-f40b-e040-e00a1806638a

(5) he New York Public Library. "Metropolitan Museum of Art -- Central Park" *The New York Public Library Digital Collections*. https://digitalcollections.nypl.org/items/510d47e0-d893-a3d9-e040-e00a18064a99

(6) The New York Public Library. "A scene during the rush hour while the strike was in progress" The New York Public Library Digital Collections. 1905. https://digitalcollections.nypl.org/items/510d47e1-061d-a3d9-e040-e00a18064a99

(7) The Miriam and Ira D. Wallach Division of Art, Prints and Photographs: Print Collection, The New York Public Library. "Bust of Mark Twain by Theresa Federowna Ries." *The New York Public Library Digital Collections*. 1897. https://digitalcollections.nypl.org/items/510d47de-85bc-a3d9-e040-e00a18064a99

(8) "Brooklyn Bridge." *Encyclopaedia Britannica*, Encyclopaedia Britannica, Inc., https://www.britannica.com/topic/Brooklyn-Bridge.

(9) "Thomas Edison: Menlo Park." *Encyclopaedia Britannica*, Encyclopaedia Britannica, Inc., https://www.britannica.com/biography/Thomas-Edison/Menlo-Park.

(10) The Miriam and Ira D. Wallach Division of Art, Prints and Photographs: Photography Collection, The New York Public Library. "Immigrant family looking for lost baggage, Ellis Island" *The New York Public Library Digital Collections*. 1905. https://digitalcollections.nypl.org/items/510d47d9-a96c-a3d9-e040-e00a18064a99

(11) The Miriam and Ira D. Wallach Division of Art, Prints and Photographs: Photography Collection, The New York Public Library. "14

St." *The New York Public Library Digital Collections*. 1891. https://digitalcollections.nypl.org/items/510d47db-92c3-a3d9-e040-e00a18064a99

(12) Schomburg Center for Research in Black Culture, Jean Blackwell Hutson Research and Reference Division, The New York Public Library. "Mayor and councilmen of Hobson City, Ala., Young Pyles, Jesse Cunningham, Edw. Pearce, Peter Doyle, S. L. Davis, Mayor, C. C. Snow." *The New York Public Library Digital Collections*. 1902. https://digitalcollections.nypl.org/items/510d47de-02f3-a3d9-e040-e00a18064a99

(13) "Astor Double Mansion on Fifth Avenue." *The Gilded Age Era*, 11 July 2012, https://thegildedageera.blogspot.com/2012/07/astor-double-mansion-on-fifth-avenue.html.

(14) The Miriam and Ira D. Wallach Division of Art, Prints and Photographs: Photography Collection, The New York Public Library. "Henry Ford, 1863 - , in his first model car 1893." *The New York Public Library Digital Collections*. 1860 - 1920. https://digitalcollections.nypl.org/items/510d47d9-3da3-a3d9-e040-e00a18064a99

(15) "Studies of Sleeping Figures for *David in Saul's Camp* (John Singer Sargent), 1937.9.16." *Harvard Art Museums Collections Online*, Harvard Art Museums, 19 Sept. 2024, https://hvrd.art/o/310505.

(16) The Miriam and Ira D. Wallach Division of Art, Prints and Photographs: Print Collection, The New York Public Library. "Jacob Riis." *The New York Public Library Digital Collections*. https://digitalcollections.nypl.org/items/99bd02cd-0814-a7c8-e040-e00a18063112

(17) Fearing, Heidi. "John D. Rockefeller." *Cleveland Historical*, 25 Aug. 2011, last updated 27 Sept. 2023, https://clevelandhistorical.org/index.php/items/show/328. Accessed 20 Sept. 2024.

"Rockefeller, John D." *Encyclopedia of Cleveland History*, Case Western Reserve University, https://case.edu/ech/articles/r/rockefeller-john-d. Accessed 20 Sept. 2024.

(18) Bain News Service, Publisher. Allison, Armour, Cornelius Vanderbilt. [Between and Ca. 1920] Photograph. Retrieved from the Library of Congress, <www.loc.gov/item/2014702721/>.

(19) **"Scott Joplin."** *Encyclopaedia Britannica*, Encyclopaedia Britannica, Inc., https://www.britannica.com/biography/Scott-Joplin. Accessed 20 Sept. 2024.

(20) **"Five Facts About Opening Night."** *Carnegie Hall*, 30 Sept. 2020, https://www.carnegiehall.org/Explore/Articles/2020/09/30/Five-Facts-About-Opening-Night. Accessed 20 Sept. 2024.

(21) The Miriam and Ira D. Wallach Division of Art, Prints and Photographs: Photography Collection, The New York Public Library. "Fifth Avenue, North west corner of 52nd Street[view of a mansion]." *The New York Public Library Digital Collections*. 1850 - 1930. https://digitalcollections.nypl.org/items/510d47e0-1cd6-a3d9-e040-e00a18064a99

COVER CITATION

H.A. Thomas & Wylie, and William Adolphe Bouguereau. H.A. Thomas & Wylie's interior view of the Hoffman House bar. [New York: H.A. Thomas & Wylie] Photograph. Retrieved from the Library of Congress, <www.loc.gov/item/2004669131/>.

Beaux, C. (1914). After the meeting [Oil on canvas]. Toledo Museum of Art. https://emuseum.toledomuseum.org/objects/54833/after-the-meeting